OOR·PLAN·
1/16" = 1:0"
ELEVATION

·SCALE·FOR·PLAN·T·ELEVATION·

10 14 18 112 116 120 124 128 132 136 140 144 148 152 156 160 164 FEET

EVATION·   ·SECTION·

E·HOUSE·

·MARYLAND·

NOTE:
FOLLOWING·ISSUE·OF·
THE·MONOGRAPH·SERIES·
WILL·CONTAIN·MEASURED·
DRAWINGS·OF·THE·INTERIOR·
OF·THE·BRICE·HOUSE·

MEAS·T·DRAWN·KENNETH·CLARK·

EARLY ARCHITECTURE
OF THE SOUTH

Other National Historical Society Publications:

THE IMAGE OF WAR: 1861–1865

TOUCHED BY FIRE: A PHOTOGRAPHIC PORTRAIT OF THE CIVIL WAR

WAR OF THE REBELLION: OFFICIAL RECORDS
  OF THE UNION AND CONFEDERATE ARMIES

OFFICIAL RECORDS OF THE UNION AND CONFEDERATE NAVIES
  IN THE WAR OF THE REBELLION

HISTORICAL TIMES ILLUSTRATED ENCYCLOPEDIA OF THE CIVIL WAR

A TRAVELLER'S GUIDE TO GREAT BRITAIN SERIES

For information about National Historical Society Publications, write:
Historical Times, Inc., 2245 Kohn Road, Box 8200, Harrisburg, Pennsylvania 17105

EARLY ARCHITECTURE OF THE SOUTH

From material originally published as
The White Pine Series of Architectural Monographs
edited by
Russell F. Whitehead and Frank Chouteau Brown

Lisa C. Mullins, Editor

Roy Underhill, Consultant

A Publication of
THE NATIONAL HISTORICAL SOCIETY

Library of Congress Cataloging-in-Publication Data

Early architecture of the South.
    (Architectural Treasures of Early America; 2)
      1. Architecture—Southern states. 2. Architecture, Colonial—Southern states. I. Mullins, Lisa C. II. Underhill, Roy. III. Series: Architectural treasures of Early America (Harrisburg, Pa.); 2.
NA720.E45   1987   720'.975   87-11070
ISBN 0-918678-21-8

The original photographs reproduced in this publication are from the collection of drawings and photographs in "The White Pine Monograph Series, Collected and Edited by Russell F. Whitehead, The George P. Lindsay Collection." The collection, part of the research and reference collections of The American Institute of Architects, Washington, D.C., was acquired by the Institute in 1955 from the Whitehead estate, through the cooperation of Mrs. Russell F. Whitehead, and the generosity of the Weyerhauser Timber Company, which purchased the collection for presentation to the Institute. The research and reference collections of the Institute are available for public use. A written request for such use is required so that space may be reserved and assistance made available.

CONTENTS

The Brickmaker's Hand

As it was intended, we stand back admiring the great homes of Charleston, Annapolis or Old Salem. The cool brick has endured fire, decay, and centuries of summer heat. But step closer, close enough that you can touch the brick of these walls. Somewhere, in one of the bricks, you will find a handprint. It may even be the smaller (yet equally work-hardened) handprint of a woman or child. Remember how these great homes began—with axes in the forest, with shovels in the clay.

A family made these bricks. Most brickmakers came to know their clay from a score of barefoot summers (and winters) helping the family work. Brickmaking in the eighteenth century remained as labor intensive as it had been in the stories of the Old Testament. Every brick, of the tens of thousands required for a building, had to be handled at least seventeen times before the builders even touched it. Some of the handling was as simple as turning a partially dried brick up on its side, repeated for each of the thousands of bricks in the drying field. Thousands of these brickmaking hands belonged to children, growing up in the trade of their ancestors.

Clay, water, fuel and a market. . . . With the right clay in the right place, a claybank might become a brickyard serving many customers. Often though, a brick home would rise from its own cellar hole. Winter was not an idle time. So much the better if the clay could be exposed to the working fingers of frost on winter nights. Through the winter too, wood for firing the brick needed to be cut. Firing the brick to make a single fireplace and chimney could consume ten cords of wood before the hearth was laid.

Tempering, as blending clay and water to the right consistency for moulding into brick is called, could be done with just hoes and shovels. With considerably more investment, they could also use a mule-driven "wheel pit." The wheel pit was simply a wagon wheel mounted on an axle that pivoted on one end, drawn in an endless circle by an ox or mule to work the clay. Apparently the effects of wagon traffic on the clay of colonial roads did not pass unnoticed.

When kept supplied with tempered clay, the brickmaker could mould 2,000 bricks a day. Filling his hands with just the right amount of clay, he would roll it and fold it into a loaf, and then slam it hard into the wooden mould to force it full to the corners. Moulds were commonly made to shape from one to four bricks. When a mould was filled (a matter of seconds) the brickmaker could scrape the excess clay off the top and flip it up on its side, ready for the off-bearers to take to the drying fields. In the field, the bearer turned the shaped clay onto the ground and returned with the empty mould for the brickmaker to refill in the ancient cycle of their labor.

From the moment the freshly moulded bricks hit the drying field, the brickmakers were at the mercy of the weather. Frost and sun could crack the bricks, a rainstorm could melt weeks of work. But that was not all. If set to dry on the bare ground, earthworms or ants emerging beneath a brick simply continued the extra three inches to the surface. Throughout the night, creatures left their tracks in the soft bricks. A racoon caused but a minor flaw, a stray cow was disaster. But never mind—the next day, as the brickmakers passed through the rows to turn the bricks, they gathered the damaged ones, tossed them back into the tempering pit and another day began.

After several days in the open air the bricks were hard enough to stack into covered piles for building into the kiln. Rather than using a fixed kiln into which they loaded the bricks, they often used a "clamp," a stack of brick arranged in such a way to form its own kiln. First they built fire tunnels or "eyes." When these were laid up, the remainder of the brick could be stacked above, about a finger-width apart. The outer walls had to be stacked tight and plastered with earth to channel the fire in the eyes through to the top of the clamp.

The first few days of burning the clamp were a test of patience. The bricks still contained enough water that they would explode if heated too fast. An extra stick thrown into the fire could produce a sound like popping popcorn—the sound of bursting bricks. For the first few days, white clouds of steam rolled from the top of the clamp. When the steam disappeared and the smoke began to run clear, the pace picked up. The crew that was already tired from tending the fires night and day, now had to feed it almost constantly to reach and maintain the 2000°F necessary to make soft clay into hard brick. Soon the fires in the eyes became so hot that a bolt of hickory tossed into it burst into flames before it landed. The top began to glow deep red with tiny hellish jets of flame. After several days the top of the clamp began to drop in the middle, the fired bricks shrinking more where the fire was hottest. The clamp emitted searing heat for days after both the fuel and the brickmakers were exhausted.

Tearing down the clamp, the brickmakers sorted their work by hardness and color. The outside brick never became hot enough to fully harden. These "samel" brick could be used only where they were protected from the weather by harder common brick from deeper in the clamp. From around the eyes, where the flames played directly on the clay, the brickmakers pulled darkly glazed clinker brick. The builder could decoratively mix these with the common brick as he laid up a wall. But that was another trade, out of the hands of the brickmakers. Their work was over, to begin again.

ROY UNDERHILL
MASTER HOUSEWRIGHT
COLONIAL WILLIAMSBURG

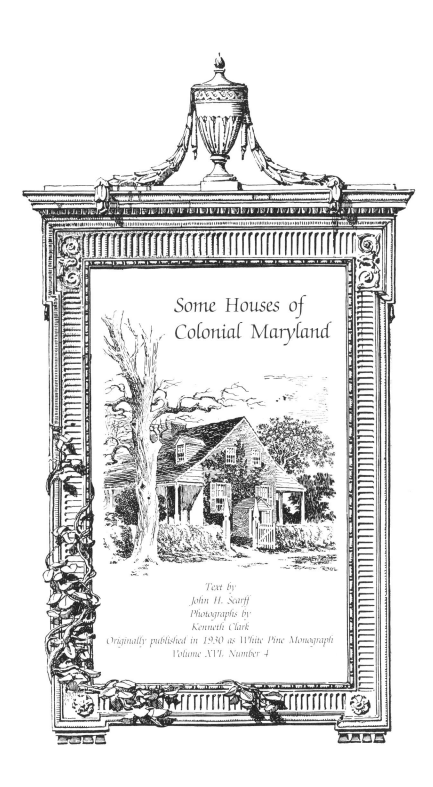

Some Houses of Colonial Maryland

Text by
John H. Scarff
Photographs by
Kenneth Clark
Originally published in 1930 as White Pine Monograph
Volume XVI, Number 4

DOWER HOUSE, NEAR MARLBORO, PRINCE GEORGE COUNTY, MARYLAND

SOME HOUSES OF COLONIAL MARYLAND

NO where is the spirit of our colonial past better preserved than in the tidewater country of Maryland and Virginia. A good life was lived and traditions of urbanity and hospitality wove themselves in the fabric of its buildings. Time has dealt gently with this district and apart from a mellowness that comes with age there has been no great change with the passing of several centuries. There is still a gracious spirit hovering over the broad waters of the Chesapeake and its estuaries and many a scene does not vary the least from the same scene when the fine brick residence whose gardens sloped in lovely terraces down to the river's edge was new and a bustling centre of prosperous enterprise. The prosperity has gone, it is true, but in its place is a simple dignity and brooding retrospect.

What constitutes the charm of our old buildings it is not difficult to say. First comes simplicity. Almost all our early houses are simple, even the finest are little more than glorified farmhouses and each and every house is eloquent of the kind of life it houses, — which is fitness or appropriateness. The materials are native, well understood, which means honesty and a certain frank courage. A sense of site contributes, for it is rare that the physical features of the landscape are not incorporated, and garden features often extend widely, achieving a happy marriage of house to land which in architecture is very near to contentment.

The traditions the early settlers to Maryland brought with them from England, the climate, and the ways of colonial life all conspired to the ends we illustrate. The settler frequently lived the life of a landed proprietor in almost feudal conditions of authority. Land was abundant and he nearly always, unlike his contemporary in New England, built in the country, away from towns. The natural functions of his household determined the plan of his house. The large central house was designed for his immediate household. Servants were plentiful and undoubtedly gay, and noisy, after their kind. What more fitting than that they and their duties be somewhat away from the family, housed in a wing. The Maryland settler was familiar, by formal education, with the classics and liked symmetry and balance. A wing corresponding to the service quarters balanced the composition and accommodated the business of the proprietor and often a school. Here he met his steward, and his dependents' children received their education. In Virginia these three departments of the household were usually housed in three independent buildings. In Maryland the climate made it convenient to connect the three elements of the architectural composition with covered passage ways. And this is the genesis of the typical Maryland Colonial plan — her first contribution to Colonial Architecture.

The Brice House in Annapolis illustrates this composite plan. (See Volume II, Chapter 3, pages 64–66.) Today it is situated on one of the narrow streets of the town but it is said that in the days of its glory the gardens fell to the river. It was the wedding gift of Thomas Jennings to Juliana Jennings and Col. James Brice in 1745. Quite recently the Baltimore Chapter of the American Institute of Architects was asked by a local newspaper to select the finest residence in the state. Although somewhat reluctant to narrow the selection to one, a vote was taken and the Brice House won first, but not undisputed, place. The result was a surprise and leads one to examine that quality of the house which entitles it to such distinction. It is now situated on a street so narrow it is almost impossible to appreciate the mass which is its most distinguished feature. Few can realize that the height of the building from the eaves to the ridge of the roof is almost as great as the height from the eaves to the first floor line. With its great central house and the two wings much lower, set at right angles, and connected by low covered passages, it is the finest expression of the distinctive Maryland plan. The façade of the main house is laid entirely in headers and not the usual Flemish bond seen in the wings. The writer ventures the criticism that the Palladian window in the second story is needlessly complicated and too crowded and, with its relieving arch cut by the cornice, is poorly composed. But withal, with its great height, beautiful fenestration and towering gable chimneys it remains one of the most effective of all Colonial houses, — a monument to some past designer of more than average taste and imagination.

The interior details are especially good. The wall panels and cornices are of plaster, the trims, chair rails and mantels of wood with carved ornamentation. The mantel brackets show most spirited carving but unfortunately the fire openings have been filled in inside the original marble facing with recent brick work. The modillioned cornice suggests an origin in the ornamental interiors of the Palazzo Massimi. The house is now the property of St. John's College and reasonably assured of a protected future of usefulness and inspiration.

Although the first settlement in Maryland was on the peninsula between the Potomac River and the Chesapeake Bay in what is now St. Mary's County, the settlements very early spread out to the north following the rivers and Bay. Calvert County, the peninsula between the Patuxent River and the Bay, was settled only a few years later. Then followed in quick succession Prince George, Anne Arundel and Charles County, all south of Baltimore. Throughout this period the waterways were the highways and practically all of the important houses were located in direct reference to the water.

An exception to this rule is the house near upper Marlboro in Prince George County, built by the Calvert Family — the Lords Proprietors of the Colony — as a hunting lodge. It is variously known as Mt. Airy or the Dower House. The original house is quite small and although it lacks the advantages of a water view, it has the favorite terraces sloping rather suddenly to the farm lands beyond. It is a simple one story brick structure with a second story in a gambrel roof. The central and taller portion is flanked by two lower wings. The façade of the main building like the Brice House is built entirely of headers. There is the local tradition that the design is one of the first ever made by Christopher Wren, when he was a boy but 14 years old. It is said he was recommended to Lord Baltimore on one of Baltimore's visits to London and was given by him the problem of designing for him, on his estate in Maryland, a hunting lodge. In proof of the tradition one's attention is called to the varying size of all doors and windows, but one fails to see why this should be attributed to inexperienced genius rather than inexperienced workmen or even time itself. The building is now much larger than the original hunting lodge, although almost all of very early origin, but unfortunately suffers greatly from neglect and a far from discriminating and wise restoration. The old place, one of the houses of the First of Maryland Colonial Families, deserves a better fate. One of the most pleasing features is the skillful junction of the two gambrel roofs. The lines are not parallel and the lower gambrel end is cut at the gable end in an unusual fashion. The small and very few dormers (or dormants, sleeping windows, as they are sometimes called by local carpenters) add character to the exterior but certainly not great comfort to the interior.

Surprising as it is to many not familiar with the houses of Maryland, the interiors of the large proportion of the houses, in spite of the small size of many of them, are often quite architectural. Some of the smallest houses boast at least one paneled room; where the detailing shows unmistakable evidences of the handicraft of workmen trained in old world traditions. Such a house is Eltonhead Manor House, built about 1690, which although it contained but six rooms, one of them is wainscoted from floor to ceiling, and shows a dentiled chair rail and cornice and a charming mantel of marked Queen Anne character. This room is now a part of the permanent collection of the Baltimore Art Museum.

Southern Maryland shows many more modest variations in wood of the traditional brick residence. These have the simple gable roof or gambrel with small and very few dormers. A characteristic trick of the chimneys is shown in Eltonhead. After the last fireplace, the chimney loses all contact with the house and rises in free and solitary height, eloquent of the early settlers fear of fire. These houses in early days were not painted, but after the Civil War, according to tradition, white-wash came into universal use as a method of cleaning up. Now these little white houses, usually inhabited by negroes, set back under old trees, have a rare charm and simple appeal, they are seldom but one room deep but often they extend in length, in varying heights, to five or six rooms.

Far from the houses already discussed and their socially homogeneous neighborhood, in Libertytown near Frederick in Western Maryland, is the charming old city residence, built by Abraham Jones about 1798. The house is now in the possession of Miss Sappington (pages 30–32). In character and detail it strongly suggests the houses of Alexandria, Virginia. The exterior bespeaks generous rooms and a gracious living, although the entrance door seems too narrow for its height and the iron rails are obviously a later addition. The interior stair spandrel shows an unusual radiating panel design and the newel seems one hundred years late, but examination fails to reveal any indication of its having been added.

All these houses are imbued with something of the same spirit and share a common quiet and modest dignity. They are of the very essence of old Maryland and silent reminders of the days and men that are gone. Those men — racy, hospitable, generous, alike in spirit and interests, proud, devoted to the good things of this world, built all of these qualities into their homes and undoubtedly agreed with Sir Henry Wotten in 1624 that: —

"Every man's proper Mansion House and Home, being the Theatre of his Hospitality, the Seat of his self Fruition, the comfortablest part of his own Life, the Noblest of his sons Inheritance, a kind of private Princedom; may, to the possessor thereof be an Epitomy of the whole World; may well deserve by these Attributes, according to the degree of the Master, to be decently and delightfully adorned."

DOWER HOUSE, NEAR MARLBORO, PRINCE GEORGE COUNTY, MARYLAND

Lord Baltimore's Shooting Lodge
DOWER HOUSE, NEAR MARLBORO, PRINCE GEORGE COUNTY, MARYLAND

HOUSE NEAR CHESTERTOWN, KENT COUNTY, MARYLAND

Window Detail
NEAR EASTON, TALBOT COUNTY, MARYLAND—BUILT ABOUT 1790

Minor Doorway
JAMES BRICE HOUSE–1740–ANNAPOLIS, MARYLAND

Main Cornice
JAMES BRICE HOUSE, ANNAPOLIS, MARYLAND

Window and Cornice
JAMES BRICE HOUSE, ANNAPOLIS, MARYLAND

Living Room Doorway
JAMES BRICE HOUSE, ANNAPOLIS, MARYLAND

Mantel in Living Room
JAMES BRICE HOUSE, ANNAPOLIS MARYLAND

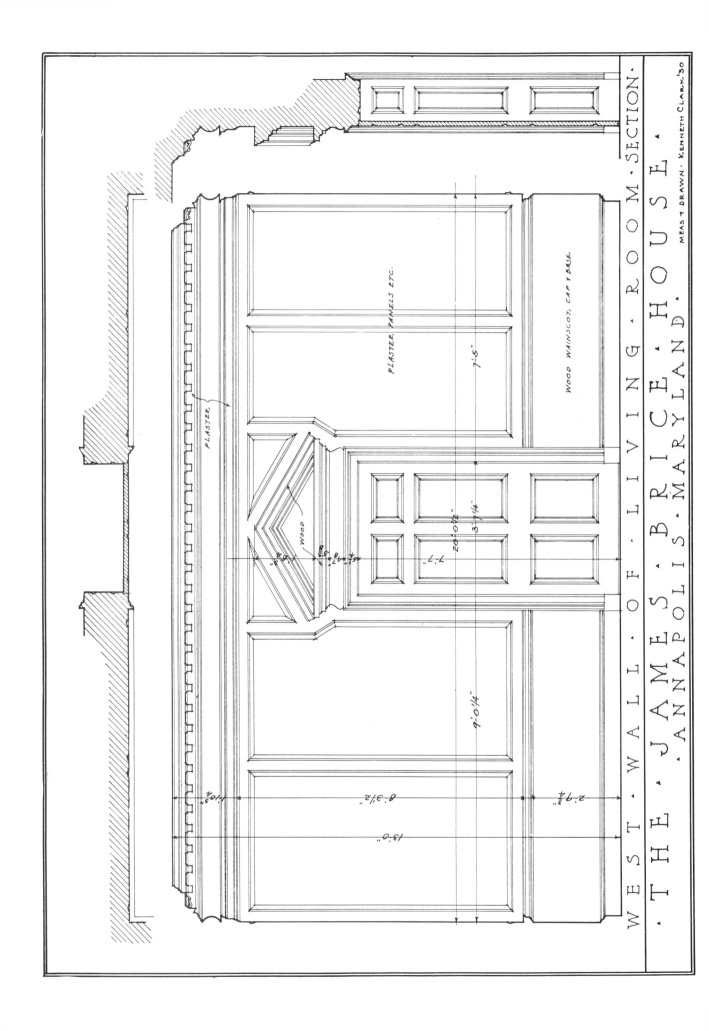

· WEST · WALL · OF · LIVING · ROOM · SECTION·

· THE · JAMES · BRICE · HOUSE ·
· ANNAPOLIS · MARYLAND ·

MEAS & DRAWN · KENNETH CLARK '30

PLASTER PANELS ETC.

WOOD WAINSCOT, CAP & BASE

PLASTER

WOOD

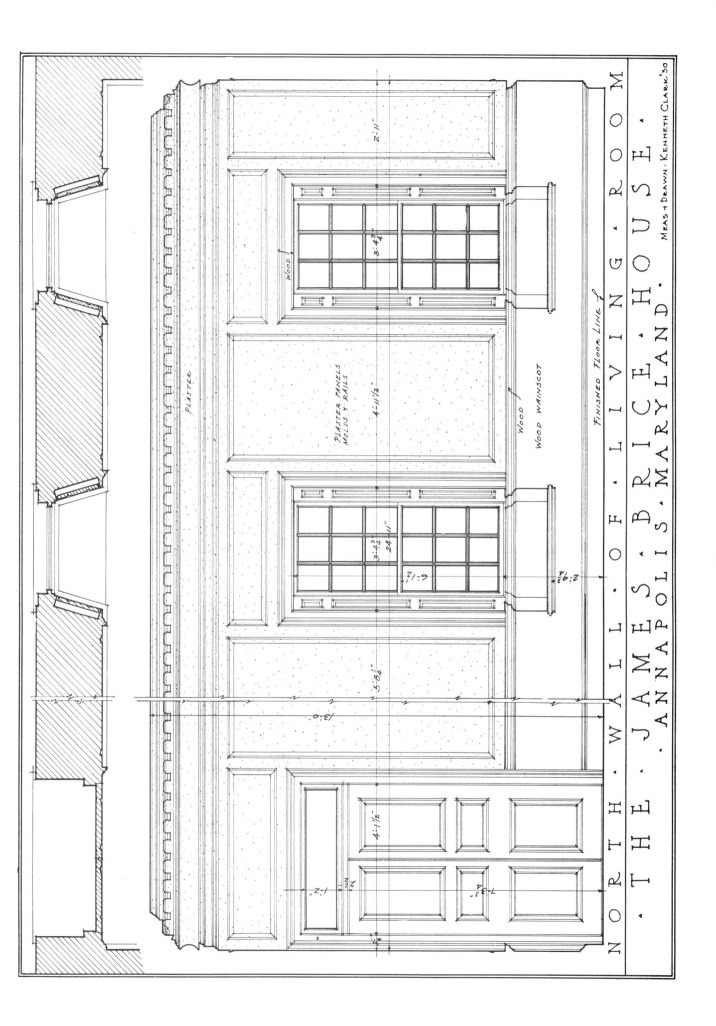

NORTH·WALL·OF·LIVING·ROOM

·THE·JAMES·BRICE·HOUSE·

·ANNAPOLIS·MARYLAND·

MEAS·+ DRAWN·KENNETH CLARK·'30

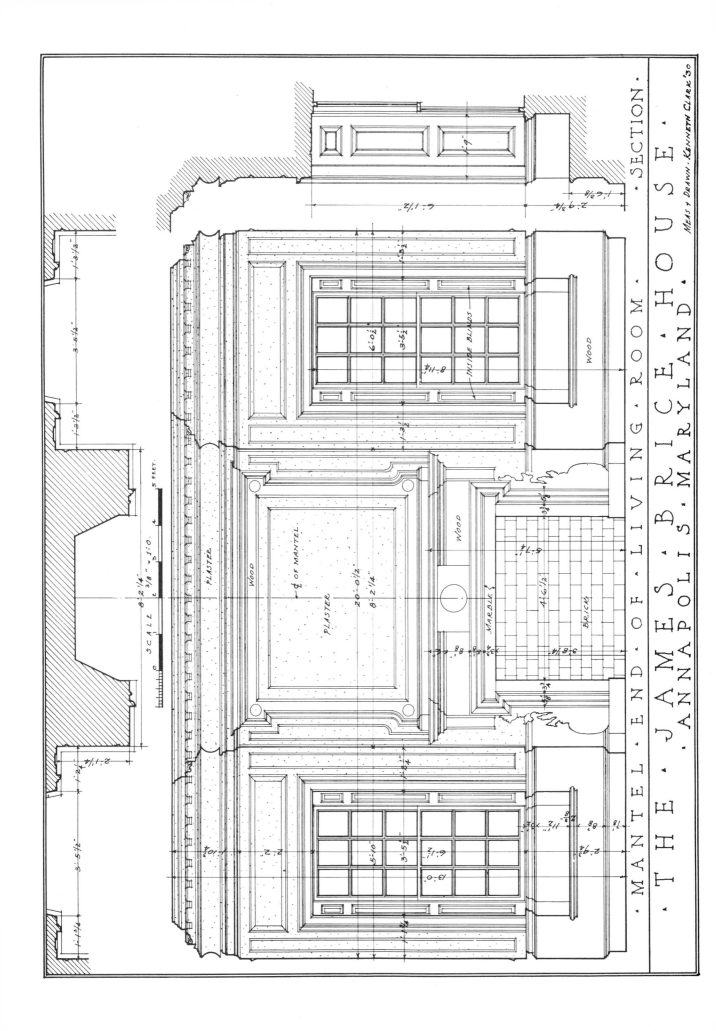

·MANTEL·END·OF·LIVING·ROOM· ·SECTION·

·THE·JAMES·BRICE·HOUSE·

·ANNAPOLIS·MARYLAND·

MEAS. & DRAWN. KENNETH CLARK '30

Living Room Mantel Wall
JAMES BRICE HOUSE, ANNAPOLIS, MARYLAND

Two Mantel Details
JAMES BRICE HOUSE, ANNAPOLIS MARYLAND

Detail Southwest Room
JAMES BRICE HOUSE, ANNAPOLIS, MARYLAND

Doorway
JONES–SAPPINGTON HOUSE, LIBERTYTOWN, FREDERICK COUNTY, MARYLAND

JONES–SAPPINGTON HOUSE, LIBERTYTOWN, FREDERICK COUNTY, MARYLAND

Stairway
JONES–SAPPINGTON HOUSE, LIBERTYTOWN, FREDERICK COUNTY, MARYLAND

JAMES BRICE HOUSE — 1740 — ANNAPOLIS, MARYLAND

Now Installed at the Baltimore Art Museum

Room Interior
ELTONHEAD MANOR— c1690–SOLOMONS, MARYLAND

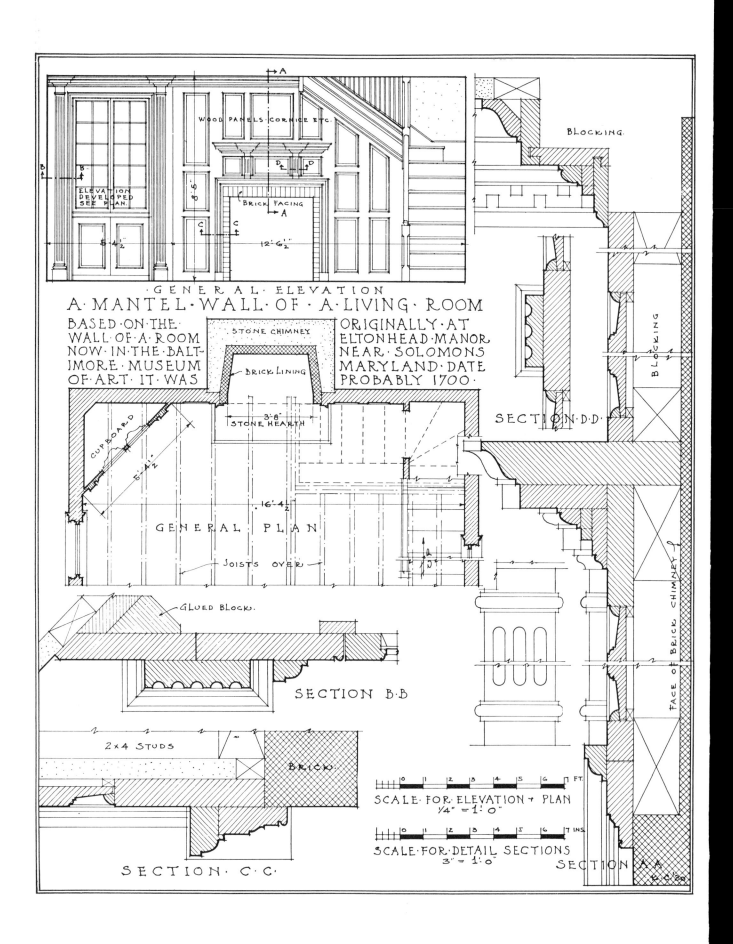

WOOD PANELS CORNICE ETC.

BLOCKING.

ELEVATION DEVELOPED SEE PLAN.

BRICK FACING

8'-5"

5'-4½"

12'-6½"

·GENERAL·ELEVATION·

A·MANTEL·WALL·OF·A·LIVING·ROOM

BASED·ON·THE·
WALL·OF·A·ROOM
NOW·IN·THE·BALT-
IMORE·MUSEUM
OF·ART·IT·WAS

ORIGINALLY·AT
ELTONHEAD·MANOR
NEAR·SOLOMONS
MARYLAND·DATE
PROBABLY·1700·

STONE CHIMNEY

BRICK LINING

BLOCKING

SECTION·D·D·

CUPBOARD

5'-4½"

3'-8"
STONE HEARTH

16'-4½"

GENERAL·PLAN

JOISTS·OVER

GLUED·BLOCK.

SECTION·B·B

FACE·OF·BRICK·CHIMNEY

2×4·STUDS

BRICK.

SCALE·FOR·ELEVATION·+·PLAN
¼"·=·1'·0"

SCALE·FOR·DETAIL·SECTIONS
3"·=·1'·0"

SECTION·C·C·

SECTION·A·A

Detail Southwest Room
JAMES BRICE HOUSE, ANNAPOLIS, MARYLAND

ACTON—c1790—ANNE ARUNDEL COUNTY, MARYLAND

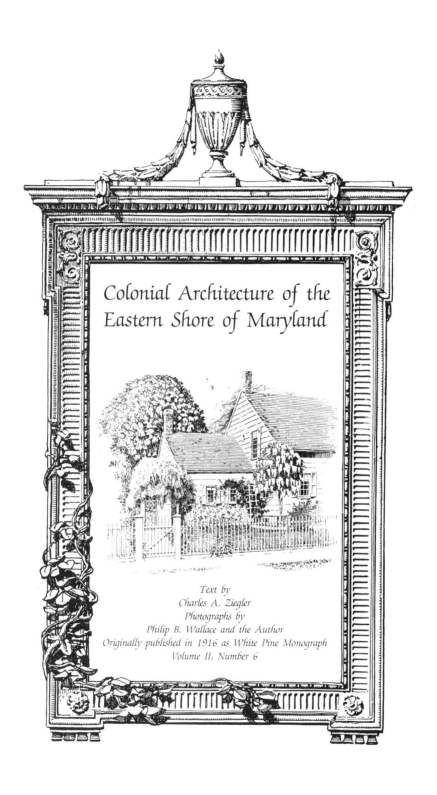

Colonial Architecture of the Eastern Shore of Maryland

Text by
Charles A. Ziegler
Photographs by
Philip B. Wallace and the Author
Originally published in 1916 as White Pine Monograph
Volume II, Number 6

Detail of Porch
BEVERLY ON THE POCOMOKE RIVER, MARYLAND
The curious treatment of the transom above the door occurs on both entrances.

COLONIAL ARCHITECTURE OF THE EASTERN SHORE OF MARYLAND

To the student of architecture who has perused the "Architectural Monograph Series" published by the White Pine Bureau, it must have become apparent that the matter has been treated from a standpoint that is quite original and refreshing. Even the closest student of the early manner of building in America must have found much that was new in the development of the styles as illustrated in the less familiar examples presented, many of which are not generally known even to the architect.

Numerous volumes have been published, illustrating the larger and more important works of the Colonial Period, but with the simpler structures, so logical and full of refinement, we are not so familiar; and yet these simpler buildings are perhaps the best evidence we have of how innate and unaffected was the art of proper building among the early colonists.

It requires no very unusual mind to compile in a fairly satisfactory manner a structure composed of odds and ends selected from that vast storehouse of accumulated "Architectural Styles," even if the fragments are used in a manner never intended by the brain that originally conceived it; but to create from very crude material, without the use of ornament and very often of mouldings, buildings that command our admiration today, bespeaks a natural and unstilted art that was popular and entirely devoid of affectation.

Victor Hugo in his "Notre Dame" states that architecture lost its function as recorder of human history in the fifteenth century when Gutenberg invented the printing press. This seems like a very abstract hypothesis and is perhaps somewhat abstruse, but his argument that before the art of printing was perfected men expressed their highest aspirations in building forms is quite sound. That architecture is crystallized history, or, as Viollet le Duc has said, "Art is the measure of civilization," is only another way of stating Hugo's eloquent argument.

Just why architecture in America deteriorated so woefully in the middle of the nineteenth century it is difficult to say, but this deterioration is itself a record of a marked change in the intellectual development of a people. In the evolution of our national life, we have reached the era where the striving for ultimate efficiency (some call it Kultur) has eliminated the art sense as a popular movement and has substituted as a lure commercial enterprise. Centering about our cities are great whirlpools of humanity that draw upon the countryside until it is barren of all but the indigent and young, and a few, very few, of those who still have visions of a golden age and dreams of a higher provincialism. There are, however, beyond the whirlpools, quiet eddies not affected by the great commotion, which although they do not gather the flotsam and jetsam of the sea, nevertheless retain that which was committed to their care in perfect contentment.

Those who have succumbed to the lure of the road feel instinctively the witchery of such environment: the long lane of spreading trees arching overhead like the vaulting in some ancient nave, with the sun-flecked roadway running between, where you raise your foot from the accelerator and permit the pulse of the motor to beat normally again; the neat whitewashed houses behind green foliage, and the kindly, slow-moving people who always seem to have so much time at their disposal.

It was in such an atmosphere as this that we found ourselves when, at the

COCKRAN'S GRANGE, NEAR MIDDLETOWN, MARYLAND

instigation of the Editor, we made the long delayed motor trip through Maryland in quest of the Colonial.

Founded in 1632 by Lord Baltimore, Maryland in many ways exhibits in its architecture the tendencies of the Cavalier stock that came with him to America to escape persecution abroad. There is no feeling of arrogance or ostentation about the work, in fact, rather a refinement that denotes gentility: but, lacking the spirit of thrift possessed by the Puritans, their houses possess a spaciousness not usually found in the North. They laid out large plantations, kept many slaves who tilled the fields and

raised the excellent thoroughbred stock; they entertained lavishly and were often ruined by their excesses, as the records show.

It is not, however, the object of this article to treat of the larger and more familiar houses, but rather of the work done on the fertile peninsula best known to the natives as the Eastern Shore of Maryland. This peninsula, sometimes referred to as the "Land of Evergreens," rich in its agricultural pursuits and ravaged very little by the wars that have raged about it, contains many quaint old towns that possess much of the charm of earlier days and innumerable old farmsteads, many of which are still owned and operated by descendants of the original settlers.

One of the most characteristic of these plantations is Beverly, situated on the Pocomoke River near the northern boundary of Virginia. Although possessing considerable architectural merit, I believe that this building has never

BOURKE HOUSE, NEAR CENTREVILLE, MARYLAND
Characteristic approach to the Maryland farmhouse.

Entrance Front

BEVERLY — 1774 — ON THE POCOMOKE RIVER, MARYLAND

been illustrated in any architectural publication before, although mentioned by several authors. It was a very pleasant surprise to me to come unexpectedly upon so excellent an example. The property has been the seat of the Dennis family of Maryland for over two hundred years. Dannock Dennis received the patent to the original estate, containing over one thousand six hundred acres, from Charles II in 1664, and it has remained the homestead of this family for nine generations.

The first house erected on the plantation was

this sort, as illustrated in the photographs of Cockran's Grange near Middletown and the Bourke House at Centreville.

In wandering through Maryland one is very much impressed by the beauty of these lanes leading up to the white farm buildings, usually so well grouped and surrounded by orchards and shade trees. The illustration of the farmhouse near Chestertown on page 45 gives some idea of the effect of these interesting white buildings among the trees. This building also conveys some idea of the simplicity of the detail and the

BEVERLY ON THE POCOMOKE RIVER, MARYLAND
The approach to this gateway is about one mile long.

destroyed by fire in the eighteenth century, the present building being erected in 1774. The old family coach with iron steps, leather springs and seats for lackeys still remains in the carriage-shed, and the old family graveyard with its stone tablets recording the passing of nine generations still nestles among the huge shade trees near the house. A broad avenue about one mile in length, flanked by large red cedars, leads to the old road at the eastern end of the plantation. These long shaded lanes are a very characteristic feature of the landscape in Maryland, even the simplest farms having splendid approaches of

excellent massing of these simple farmhouses.

Many of the smaller houses seen along the roadside might well serve as models for the moderate-sized houses that are being erected throughout the country in such atrociously bad taste: in fact, one is strongly impressed by the superiority of the crudest negro quarters in Maryland as compared with the average mechanic's home in more progressive sections. The roofs are always just the right pitch with only cornice enough to perform the proper functions of a cornice, and these with very simple mouldings, if any. The cornice was seldom

FARMHOUSE NEAR WESTOWN, MARYLAND

EARLY FARMHOUSE ON MARYLAND STATE ROAD

OLD SLAVE QUARTERS ON MARYLAND STATE ROAD

STEPHENS HOUSE, GALENA, MARYLAND

OLD HOUSE NEAR KINGSTON, MARYLAND

OLD FARMHOUSE NEAR CHESTERTOWN, MARYLAND

OLD HOUSE NEAR CECILTON, MARYLAND

Showing characteristic method of enlarging the building from generation to generation.

carried up the gable ends, these being usually finished with a face-board over which the shingles project slightly. The chimneys were always of brick and usually very generous in size. The gambrel roof is seldom seen in this section. In enlarging the houses it was usual to prolong the main axis of the building, producing long, low lines with roofs at different levels. Very often the addition was larger than the original building, as in the old house near Cecilton, above, where we have three distinct divisions, the smaller section being probably the original. Sometimes, however, wings were carried out to the rear, as in the old house near Kingston, below, but the treatment of the intersection of the roofs and grouping of gables was always somewhat similar and forms one of the charms of these simple buildings.

OLD HOUSE NEAR KINGSTON, MARYLAND

Another example showing interesting development of additions.

OLD HOUSE IN CHESTERTOWN, MARYLAND

This quaint old town was the original port of entry for Maryland before Baltimore was chosen and contains many excellent houses built during the early part of the eighteenth century.

The Stephens House at Galena, page 44, formerly Georgetown Cross Roads, was originally a log cabin and is reputed to be two hundred years old. As was very often the case where the early settlers became more prosperous and sought more commodious surroundings, the building was extended and the entire construction covered with white pine siding, and with this protection many excellent examples of the first houses erected in this country have been preserved.

The road running past this building is a portion of the Maryland State Road, which runs the entire length of the Eastern Shore and is one of the most excellent roads imaginable and one that the architectural student might profitably make use of if he would see evidence of the fact that a proper sense of proportion was a common heritage in the early days of our history, and not possessed solely by the designers of the more pretentious Georgian examples.

TWO OLD FARMHOUSES NEAR POCOMOKE CITY, MARYLAND
It is interesting to note curious fenceposts which show the English influence.

TEACKLE HOUSE, PRINCESS ANNE, MARYLAND

This house was made famous in the story of "The Curtailed Hat" by George Alfred Townsend.

Detail of River Entrance
BEVERLY ON THE POCOMOKE RIVER, MARYLAND
The ironwork was brought from England about 1775. The arched
device for carrying the lantern ring over the steps is very unusual.

Annapolis on the Severn

Text by
Delos Smith
Photographs by
Kenneth Clark
Originally published in 1929 as White Pine Monograph
Volume XV, Number 6

Looking Toward State House Circle
MARYLAND STATE HOUSE—1772—ANNAPOLIS, MARYLAND

ANNAPOLIS ON THE SEVERN

TURNING back in the history of Annapolis to the early period before the great houses were built, we reconstruct a picture which might be entitled — the town with a future. The first settled areas are marked by modest clusters of buildings with wide unoccupied acres between, through which embryonic streets have been cut. The center of the peninsula is high ground upon which the seat of government is established with church adjoining. The principal streets radiate to the waterfront along Spa Creek and the Severn River. On the former lies the large estate of Carrollton and just upstream is Acton, the first land grant hereabouts. The entire waterfront is reserved for building sites save only for the dock which faces the harbor. In the triangular area based upon the dock and rising to Church Circle lie the shops, storehouses, and smaller dwellings, the latter steep-roofed like plantation houses and varied only occasionally by larger two-storied structures. The Carroll and Tasker estates of Spa Creek are thus cut off by the business of Main Street from the easterly dwelling area along Prince George Street where early settlers like Jennings, Dorsey, and Brewer have established their homes facing toward the river.

Traffic hums about the dock where hogsheads of tobacco rolling in from the counties are jostled by alluring bales of merchandise from over the sea. There is a steady influx of new colonists and it is evident that the older houses resting here so picturesquely amid their foliage are soon to have fine neighbors. When they have all come and their fine houses have been built our panorama will turn to another period in which the completed city shows a fascinating picture of Renaissance luxury; in Annapolis it is called "The Golden Age."

So much of the early period is gone that reconstruction is difficult. For example the first governor's mansion built on Cornhill Street for Francis Nicholson (1694–9) has become only a memory, and the first church, the first state house, the first armory are known only by fragmentary descriptions. The architecture of the mid-eighteenth century has been more fortunate. Beginning with Governor Ogle, who came out in 1732 and served intermittently over a period of twenty years, the proprietary governors took a leading part in the development of architecture. Governor Ogle's House, built about 1742, stands today as evidence of his good taste in building. His son inherited the house and made various additions, one of which may have been the octagonal wing at the rear, as shown on page 68. One is led to believe that Governor Ogle also built in 1757 the splendid country mansion of Belair in Prince George's County and certainly in his time the first part of the Carroll House (1735) was built, as well as the Brice House (1740), and the Bordley and the Jennings Houses.

The Carroll House, of which the southerly facade is shown on page 55, represents more than one period of colonial building but the additions were ever in keeping with the original so that it presents today a unified picture of large and lordly mansion. True, the plan lacks dignity because of the crowded stair hall and narrowed circulations; yet, its lofty mass and good brickwork show how a fine building may be accomplished by simple means. The segmental arches are among the few in Annapolis.

The Brice House is like Carrollton in that it faces south; generally the houses are turned obliquely to the principal points of the compass with the result that every side gets the sun. Back of the Brice House and probably over twenty years later than it in date of erection is the Paca House, now a famous hotel. On page 56 is a rare view showing the old mansion as it stood before alteration. As the home of William Paca, a Signer of the Declaration of Independence, it holds an unusual interest. In point of design there can be little doubt of its debt to the older home of the Brices, that first grand house which heralded the dawn of "The Golden Age" and set the style for so many mansions to come.

Returning to governors and governors' mansions, we discover that McDowell Hall, the present main building of St. John's College, was originally erected as "Government House" during the term of Thomas Bladen, governor from 1742 to 1747. The site selected was on the open ground toward Dorsey's Creek north of the State House which had been built about the year 1700 with W. Bladen as architect. Construction on the new government house started in 1745 but the governor had conceived it on so expensive a scale that the House of Burgesses objected to the cost and finally refused further appropriations. At this point, it is said, the walls were up and the rafters in place; but work was stopped perforce for lack of funds and thus the building stood a skeleton open to the winds for forty years. The dream of Duff, the architect, who is said to have brought out the plans with him from Scotland, remained unrealized until another architect, probably Robert Key, finished the building for the uses of St. John's College. And thus, with the addition of a later cupola, it stands today: dour, Caledonian, and uncompromising—as was doubtless the governor in his dealings with the burgesses.

With this exception however architectural projects were fostered in a harmonious atmosphere. In the case of Governor Sharpe and the people we find only considerateness on the one hand and unbounded popularity on the other. It has remained for an Englishwoman, Lady Edgar, to tell the story of the period; and, from the present antiquarian activity of St. John's College, it is evident that the architectural records of neglected Annapolis are at last to be compiled. As between the earlier and the later work a difference must be kept in mind, namely, that the earlier was more individual and in a sense experimental while the later work held close to an accepted style, established in days of opulence when society realized itself. English architecture was the vogue while English political loyalties were fading; but the personality of Governor Sharpe was such as to pacify the political belligerents throughout the province. Long before the Stamp Act battle of 1765 which took place within sight of his Annapolis mansion he might have known that the American temper was tending toward revolution and yet his patronage was lent to the peaceful development of a loyal colony and his friends were the builders of the fine mansions of the period.

John Ridout was secretary to the governor and came out with him in 1753. Seven years later at the age of twenty-eight he completed the house which stands today beautifully preserved on Duke of Gloucester Street facing the old mansion of Carrollton. Some of the best elements of the mature period are realized in its design; see page 61 and 62. The wings, but faintly reminiscent of their remote progenitors of the English manor house, are truly Annapolitan; rather detached in composition and projecting to the front. The refined windows, the scholarly doorway, and the plain brick belt course are features in a memorable façade the effect of which is heightened by the delicate pattern of the "all header" bond, peculiar to Annapolis but used first about 1650 in Governor Calvert's country house, Mount Airy, in Prince George's County. In plan the Ridout House is like the Brice and Randall Houses in that the front door is not on center of the hall. On either hand is a fine room, with stair seen through a graceful archway. At the rear are drawing and dining rooms overlooking the terraced garden from which, see pages 59 and 60, we are privileged to see the intimate side of the house and the Palladian window which *intersects the cornice!* Attempt, modern architects, if you dare such an amazing feat of design; and achieve if you can such a happy result!

Less fortunate in preservation is the house of Dr. Upton Scott, another friend and contemporary of Governor Sharpe: see pages 69, 70, 71, 72 and 76. It stands back from Shipwright Street facing Spa Creek and lacks the wings with which most of the local mansions were provided. Its age is probably little less than that of the Ridout House but, failing the care which that family has ever given to its ancestral home, the Scott House has lost much in quality. One prefers to think of it as shown in old pictures taken before it was shuttered and painted and before its long garden wall was removed. The singular simplicity of the plan awakes a suspicion that the designer was actuated by the practical needs of a physician's house rather than by the more intangible values of architecture.

Governor Eden who held office from 1769 until the war, lived for a time at the Scott House, and it may be that he entertained his friend, George Washington, here. At all events he was patron and friend of the architect, Robert Key, and generally exercised a friendly influence on architecture even when the colonists were turning toward independence. In his time the Chase House was built, and the Hammond House (Volume VIII, Chapters 3 and 4) and present State House commenced.

The Chase House motives are perhaps as well known as any in Annapolis, see pages 57 and 58. It is lofty and manorial: the English manor house in type but built by an American patriot. The plan shows that wings were originally intended; but they were never built. In view of this fact we find the conception of the façade to be nearly identical with Winslow Hall in Buckinghamshire, England, which was erected about the year 1700. The coincidence is but one of many which might be traced. In each case of similarity we find that the American building followed but slowly the English original with an interval of two or three generations between. In plan also, but with smaller dimensions, the Chase House follows the precedent of Renaissance manor houses in the mother country. It is unique in Annapolis but unfortunately without garden setting; would that it might have been built in the earlier day when so many Annapolis acres were undeveloped, when it was only "a town with a future."

By the time the war began, Governor Eden was forced to leave and the period was completed—the future realized. Fortunately for us the city has lain ever since in the amber of inspiring precedent and graceful memory. In the search for American backgrounds it furnishes a field that appeals no less to the reason than to the sentiment. Peculiarly rich in the charm of colonial settlement, it furnishes a living memorial of things that are human and universal—the substance from which architecture is made.

CARROLL HOUSE, SPA CREEK, ANNAPOLIS, MARYLAND

WILLIAM PACA HOUSE, PRINCE GEORGE STREET, ANNAPOLIS, MARYLAND

Now Carvel Hall Hotel

SAMUEL CHASE HOUSE, CORNER OF MARYLAND AVENUE & KING GEORGE STREET, ANNAPOLIS, MARYLAND

Entrance Detail
CHASE HOUSE, MARYLAND AVENUE, ANNAPOLIS, MARYLAND

Detail of Garden Entrance
JOHN RIDOUT HOUSE, ANNAPOLIS, MARYLAND

Garden Elevation

JOHN RIDOUT HOUSE, ANNAPOLIS, MARYLAND

JOHN RIDOUT HOUSE, DUKE OF GLOUCESTER STREET, ANNAPOLIS, MARYLAND

Detail of Main Façade and Flanking Wing
JOHN RIDOUT HOUSE, ANNAPOLIS, MARYLAND

Front Elevation

BRICE HOUSE–1740–CORNER EAST AND PRINCE GEORGE STREET, ANNAPOLIS, MARYLAND

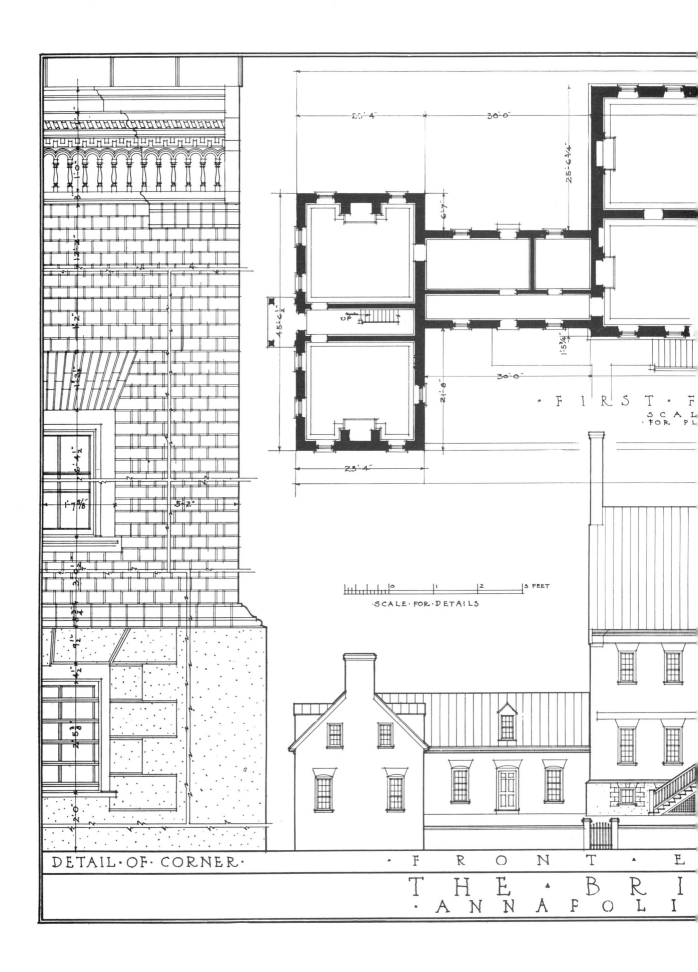

DETAIL·OF·CORNER·

·SCALE·FOR·DETAILS·

·FIRST·F
SCAL
FOR·PL

·F R O N T · E

T H E · B R I

· A N N A P O L I

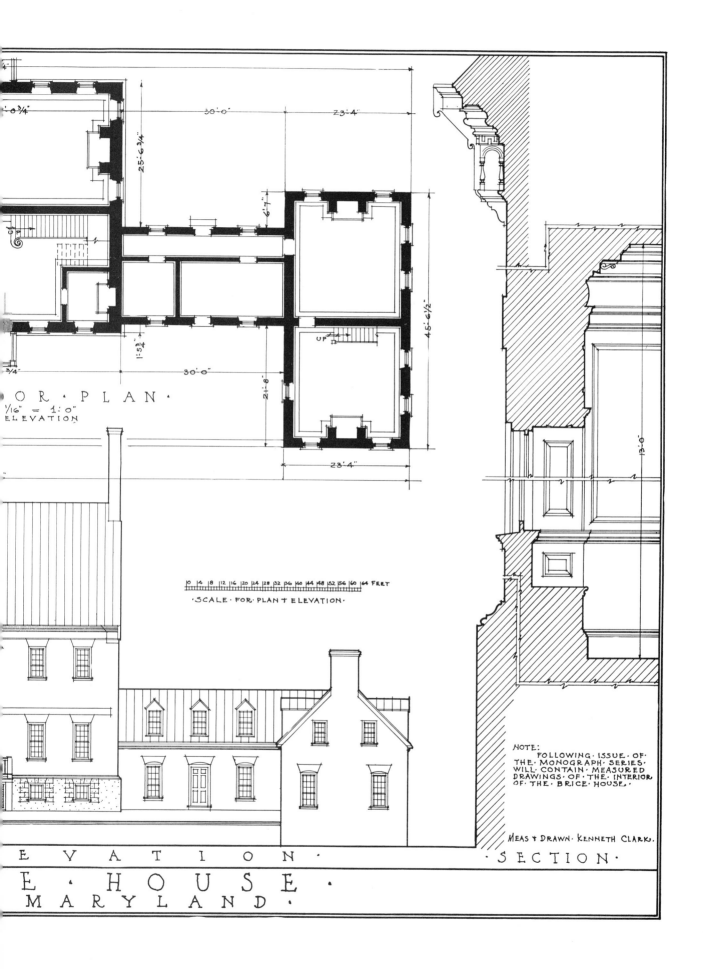

·OR·PLAN·
1/16" = 1:0"
ELEVATION

30'-0"   23'-4"

25'-6¾"

6'-7"

45'-6½"

1'-5¾"

30'-0"   21'-8"

23'-4"

|0 |4 |8 |12 |16 |20 |24 |28 |32 |36 |40 |44 |48 |52 |56 |60 |64 FEET
·SCALE·FOR·PLAN ┼ ELEVATION·

13'-0"

NOTE:
FOLLOWING·ISSUE·OF·
THE·MONOGRAPH·SERIES·
WILL·CONTAIN·MEASURED·
DRAWINGS·OF·THE·INTERIOR·
OF·THE·BRICE·HOUSE·

MEAS ┼ DRAWN·KENNETH CLARK·

EVATION·   ·SECTION·

E·HOUSE·
MARYLAND·

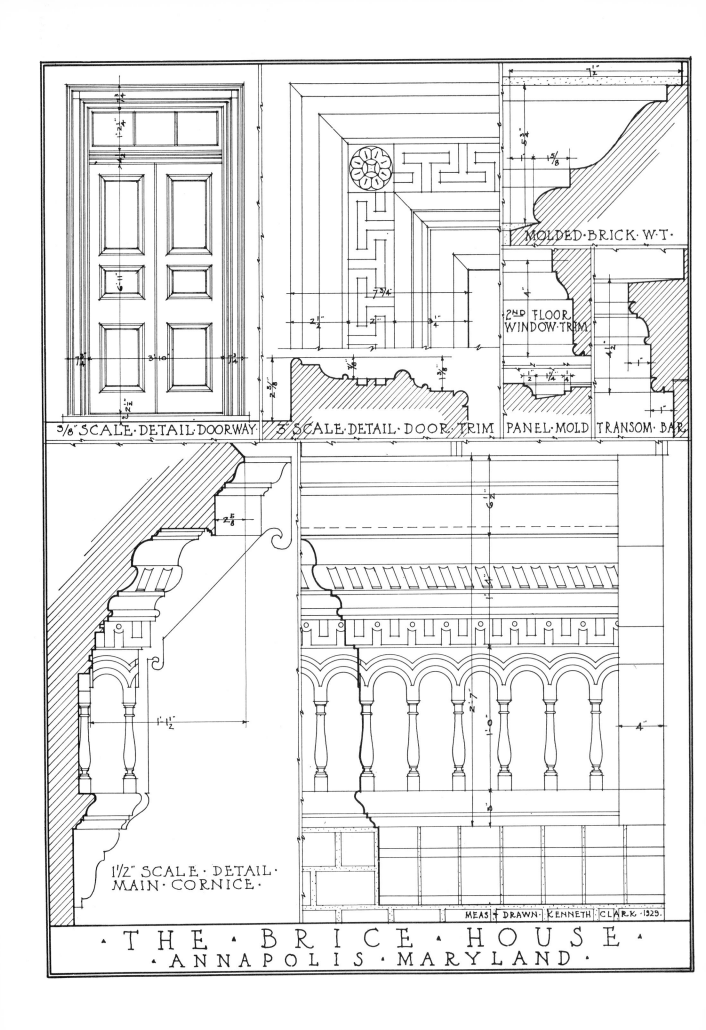

3/8" SCALE · DETAIL · DOORWAY

3" SCALE · DETAIL · DOOR · TRIM

PANEL · MOLD

TRANSOM · BAR

MOLDED · BRICK · W·T·

2ND FLOOR WINDOW · TRIM

1½" SCALE · DETAIL ·
MAIN · CORNICE ·

MEAS + DRAWN · KENNETH · CLARK · 1929.

· T H E · B R I C E · H O U S E ·
· A N N A P O L I S · M A R Y L A N D ·

McDOWELL HALL, ST. JOHN'S COLLEGE, ANNAPOLIS, MARYLAND
Thos. Bladen, fifth Royal Governor of Maryland began this building in 1745 for a Governor's palace.
It stood unfinished for many years.

Detail of Doorway in Octagonal Wing at the Rear
OGLE HOUSE, 33 COLLEGE AVENUE, ANNAPOLIS, MARYLAND
Residence of Governor Samuel Ogle 1747–1752

Detail of Entrance Doorway
DR. UPTON SCOTT HOUSE, SHIPWRIGHT STREET, ANNAPOLIS, MARYLAND
Now a home of the Sisters of Notre Dame

Garden Elevation

DR. UPTON SCOTT HOUSE, SHIPWRIGHT STREET, ANNAPOLIS, MARYLAND

Main Stairway

DR. UPTON SCOTT HOUSE, SHIPWRIGHT STREET, ANNAPOLIS MARYLAND

Entrance Hall
DR. UPTON SCOTT HOUSE, SHIPWRIGHT STREET, ANNAPOLIS, MARYLAND

Georgian Stairway
BRICE HOUSE, ANNAPOLIS, MARYLAND

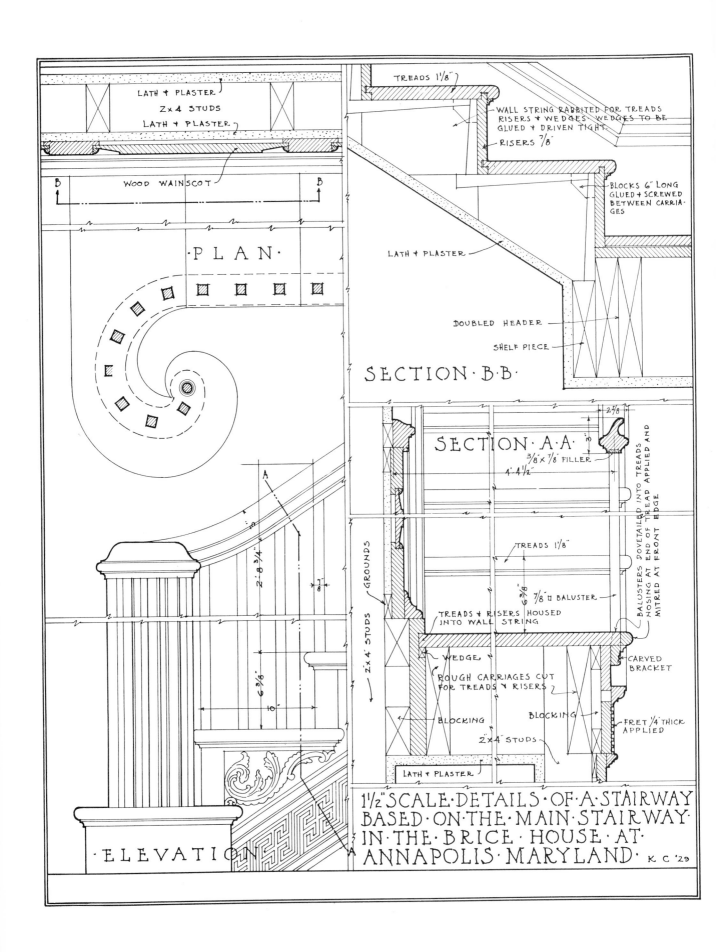

LATH + PLASTER

2 x 4 STUDS

LATH + PLASTER

TREADS 1⅛"

WALL STRING RABBITED FOR TREADS
RISERS + WEDGES WEDGES TO BE
GLUED + DRIVEN TIGHT

RISERS ⅞"

·PLAN·

B

B

WOOD WAINSCOT

BLOCKS 6" LONG
GLUED + SCREWED
BETWEEN CARRIAGES

LATH + PLASTER

DOUBLED HEADER

SHELF PIECE

SECTION·B·B·

A

SECTION·A·A·

2⅝"

3"

3/8 x ⅞" FILLER

4'-4½"

A

2'-8¾"

TREADS 1⅛"

GROUNDS

6⅜"

⅞" □ BALUSTER

BALUSTERS DOVETAILED INTO TREADS
NOSING AT END OF TREAD APPLIED AND
MITRED AT FRONT EDGE

7/8"

6⅜"

10"

2 x 4 STUDS

TREADS + RISERS HOUSED
INTO WALL STRING

WEDGE

ROUGH CARRIAGES CUT
FOR TREADS + RISERS

BLOCKING

BLOCKING

2 x 4 STUDS

LATH + PLASTER

CARVED
BRACKET

FRET ¼ THICK
APPLIED

·ELEVATION·

1½" SCALE · DETAILS · OF · A · STAIRWAY
BASED · ON · THE · MAIN · STAIRWAY
IN · THE · BRICE · HOUSE · AT ·
ANNAPOLIS · MARYLAND · K C '29

Window Detail
BRICE HOUSE, ANNAPOLIS, MARYLAND

Detail of Hall
DR. UPTON SCOTT HOUSE, SHIPWRIGHT STREET, ANNAPOLIS, MARYLAND

Domestic Architecture of Anne Arundel County, Maryland

Text by
Arthur C. Holden
Photographs by
Kenneth Clark
Originally published in 1931 as White Pine Monograph
Volume XVII, Number 5

CEDAR PARK, ANNE ARUNDEL COUNTY, MARYLAND

DOMESTIC ARCHITECTURE OF
ANNE ARUNDEL COUNTY, MARYLAND

ON the western shore of Chesapeake Bay in Anne Arundel County, Maryland, many houses, masterpieces of design, survive from the period preceding the Revolution. Some of them have been greatly changed to meet the necessities or whims of a long line of occupants, but even beneath disfiguring alterations can be seen the true beauty of one of the great periods of American architecture.

Probably one of the finest houses of Anne Arundel County is Tulip Hill, recently restored and now owned by Mrs. Henry H. Flather of Washington, D.C., through whose courtesy it is included in this chapter. It is picturesquely situated on the edge of a bluff with terraces falling off to the water. The general plan is of the type frequently found in tidewater Maryland and Virginia, but uniquely developed. The large central part has a roof that is both hipped and gambreled. The original house was built by Samuel Galloway in 1745. The wings which make it a true manorial type were added about forty years later.

The entrance is on the north side and this façade is formal and evenly balanced. In all probability, the entrance porch was added at a considerably later date. The southern façade of the house is far more informal. The window spacings are irregular, and a delightful hood shelters the entrance door.

An interesting feature of the plan is the irregular arrangement of the interior rooms within the rectangle of the walls. The hall running through the house with the double arch framing the stair alcove and door to the rear terrace is a feature of great charm. The varied size drawing and reception rooms open out of this hall. The stairs are especially noted for their graceful proportions and the ease and comfort of the rise.

There is a great deal of interesting carving about both exterior and interior. The inserts in the pediment on the entrance front are most unusual. Even though of later date, the little wooden cherub over the porch shows to what charming lengths this fondness for ornament can be carried, when once introduced. The carving on the hood over the terrace door is particularly naive. The ends of the stair treads, probably designed on the job by a master craftsman, are one of the loveliest examples known. The beautiful shell top

cabinet in the entrance hall has been placed in a unique position at an angle at the foot of the stairs.

There are many refinements in the design. For example, the brackets in the front cornice are not repeated at the rear of the house. The brickwork on the main house is in Flemish bond, but American bond has been used in the wings. There is a projecting course of brick, frequently found in both Maryland and Virginia houses, between the first and second floor windows of the main house which is repeated in the wings though reduced in size.

It is also interesting to note that the splayed flat arches of ground brick usually found over the windows of the great houses of this period are omitted over the windows of the main house. The brick is laid directly on the wood frames with only a header course marking the openings. In the later wings, however, the brick arches were used in the lower story.

There has been much discussion about the brick used in colonial Maryland and Virginia and there is a tradition that much of it was brought from England. The facing brick on Tulip Hill was probably imported, but an old account book now in the possession of Miss Murray of Ivy Neck, one of the family who came into the ownership of the house, carries the following items entered by Samuel Galloway.

"By making and laying in my house, 124,938 bricks at 20 shillings—£124 18s 9p. By making 18,000 bricks at 4 shillings—£3 16s, as per agreement." These brick mentioned were evidently used for backings of the main walls and for the interior partitions and chimneys.

An older house than Tulip Hill is Cedar Park which was built by Richard Galloway about 1700. There is a record that he assumed the title to the property in 1697. The house as it stands today has many alterations, though the steepness of the roof immediately proclaims its real date. The original chimneys were built outside the end walls. It is probable that the low section at the rear is one of the later additions. When this was constructed, it was built out flush with the chimney. With two hundred years of weathering, the brick has not been impervious to storms and large portions of the walls have been stuccoed over as a protection. Some of this stucco has now been removed showing the English bond in the ends, although part of the main house is still covered with stucco, including the interesting corner pilasters.

Tudor Hall is also a very old house that has suffered many alterations although it still retains a good deal of charm. It was constructed by Edward Hall in 1722. There is a record that one of the wings was removed bodily to the nearby town of Owensville. Certainly the two story porch is a much later addition and there is evidence that the façade of the central part was probably rebuilt in the early 1800's.

Sudley also shows great age in the steepness of the roof and in the interior detail. The woodwork in the principal room is a fine example executed in a strong and bold scale. The large original window panes and the old paneled door which is still visible under the jig-saw porch, added in the President Hayes period, are details which proclaim the merit of this fine old house.

St. James Church is one of many old brick churches of tidewater Maryland and Virginia. There is a gravestone in the yard which bears the date 1663 though the building was probably slightly later. The main front is composed entirely of header bricks. This type of church suggests that these buildings may have been executed from stock plans or by workmen who progressed from town to town. A tradition persists that Queen Anne donated money to build a church every ten miles in Anne Arundel County.

The Sellman Homestead is a bona fide example of the original old frame farmhouse constructed with massive exterior chimneys built outside the walls. Of course, the dormer and porch are modern additions. There is a naive informality in the method in which the out buildings have been linked up with the main house in a manner which we are accustomed to associate more with New Hampshire, but which is frequently found in the earlier houses of tidewater Maryland. The farm wings are picturesque because of this irregularity and informality. The break in the clapboarding is accounted for by the fact that the last wing was apparently moved up from another location as close to the old house as possible and the space between the chimney and the new wing filled in by patch work on the exterior, thus providing a closet within the space in the reveal of the chimney.

Lothian is a brick house of later date than the other buildings illustrated in this chapter. The left side of the house was built in 1804 by Phillip Thomas. The right side was added about 1840. The house is now owned by Miss Sally Hall, direct descendant of the original builder. The location is near Mt. Zion in typical, rolling farm country. The house is an interesting example of the use of stock designs by the early builders and it is one of several instances where apparently the plan of an English type city house was used. Examples exist where the parapet walls are continued up through the roof as would have been done in London, although in Lothian this is not the case. Limestone lintels are used over the windows in place of the earlier splayed ground brick arches though the latter have been used in the cellar windows. The entrance door is typical of many, but developed with an individuality and playfulness that indicate an intelligent craftsman on the job.

The city of Annapolis, also located in Anne Arundel County, contains many fine examples of work of the Colonial Period which have been dealt with in previous chapters. However, included in this number is a photograph of an unusual brick-ended wing of an old house on Main and Conduit streets, Annapolis. The large chimney, the narrow proportions of the end, the row lock arch windows and the projecting brick courses marking off the stories are features that give a peculiar charm to this old building. Unusual proportions are frequently responsible for a subtle attraction that is achieved in no other way.

We know that the colonial builders were master craftsmen and that the knowledge of the workmen on the job, in regard to design, was far superior to that possessed by any of our workmen today. Modern inventions and modern improvements, of course, were lacking and there were many faults of structural design, such as the wide spacing of heavy beams, the placing of wood work where liable to the effect of dampness without proper protection. These were faults which have caused deterioration and decay, but with them all we are nevertheless forced to accord to the colonial builders a very high place as masters not only of design, but also of construction.

It would be interesting for us today to know more of how the traditions of good design were preserved and disseminated in colonial days. We seldom find any remnants of the buildings of that period which are faulty in either mass, line or detail. Whether taste on the part of the general public was at a higher level or whether this superiority of design was due to the better training and higher culture of the craftsmen, it is impossible for us to tell. Could we glean from the past this one secret it might revolutionize the character of the modern American home. Certainly to those who study the methods and the achievements of the early builders a real reward is to be found in the consciousness that in our own country such high traditions and standards at one time prevailed.

ST. JAMES CHURCH, ANNE ARUNDEL COUNTY, MARYLAND

SUDLEY, ANNE ARUNDEL COUNTY, MARYLAND

CEDAR PARK, ANNE ARUNDEL COUNTY, MARYLAND

WOOD

CEMENT STEPS

·DETAIL·OF·DOORWAY·

SCALE·FOR·DETAILS·

SCALE·FOR·ELEVATION·

"LOTHIAN"·ANNE·ARUNDEL·COUNTY·MARYLAND

Detail of Entrance Doorway
LOTHIAN, ANNE ARUNDEL COUNTY, MARYLAND

LOTHIAN, ANNE ARUNDEL COUNTY, MARYLAND
Original house built 1804.

TUDOR HALL, ANNE ARUNDEL COUNTY, MARYLAND
Original house built 1722.

Front Elevation

SELLMAN HOMESTEAD, ANNE ARUNDEL COUNTY, MARYLAND

South Elevation

TULIP HILL, ANNE ARUNDEL COUNTY, MARYLAND

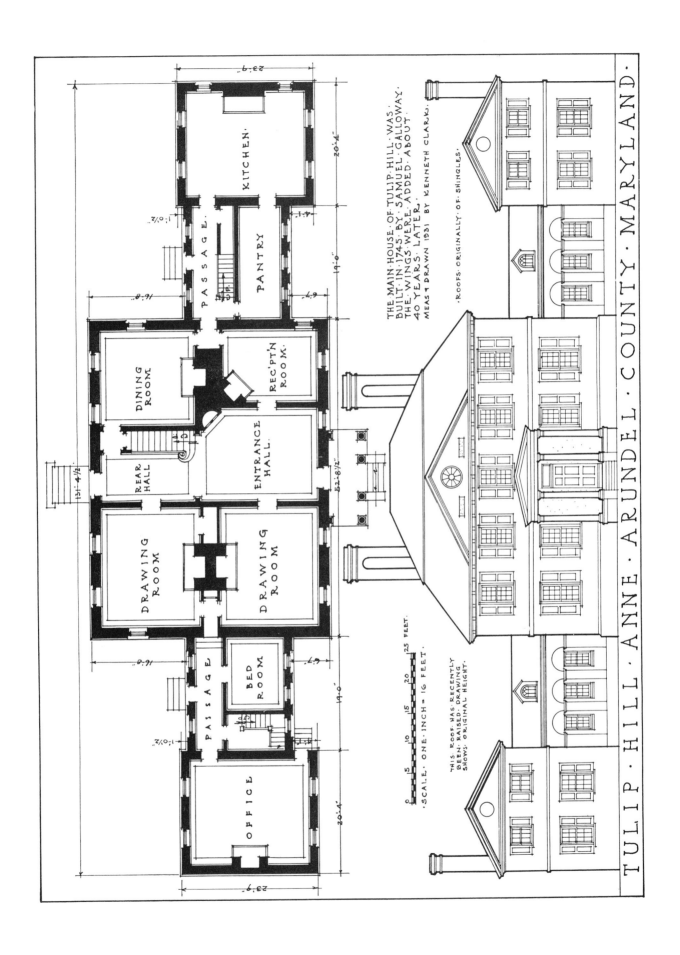

KITCHEN.

PANTRY

PASSAGE.

23'-9"

20'-4"

1'-0½"

1'-4"

14'-0"

5'-7"

16'-0"

DINING
ROOM

REC'PT'N
ROOM.

REAR
HALL

ENTRANCE
HALL.

DRAWING
ROOM

DRAWING
ROOM

131'-4½"

51'-8½"

BED
ROOM

OFFICE

PASSAGE

16'-0"

5'-7"

1'-0½"

14'-0"

20'-4"

23'-9"

THE·MAIN·HOUSE·OF·TULIP·HILL·WAS·
BUILT·IN·1745·BY·SAMUEL·GALLOWAY·
THE·WINGS·WERE·ADDED·ABOUT·
40·YEARS·LATER.
MEAS'd DRAWN 1931 BY KENNETH CLARK.

·ROOFS·ORIGINALLY·OF·SHINGLES·

0 5 10 15 20 25 FEET.
·SCALE·ONE·INCH=16 FEET·

THIS·ROOF·HAS·RECENTLY·
BEEN·RAISED·DRAWING·
SHOWS·ORIGINAL·HEIGHT·

·TULIP·HILL·ANNE·ARUNDEL·COUNTY·MARYLAND·

North Elevation

TULIP HILL, ANNE ARUNDEL COUNTY, MARYLAND

Detail of North Elevation
TULIP HILL, ANNE ARUNDEL COUNTY, MARYLAND

Detail of South Doorway
TULIP HILL, ANNE ARUNDEL COUNTY, MARYLAND

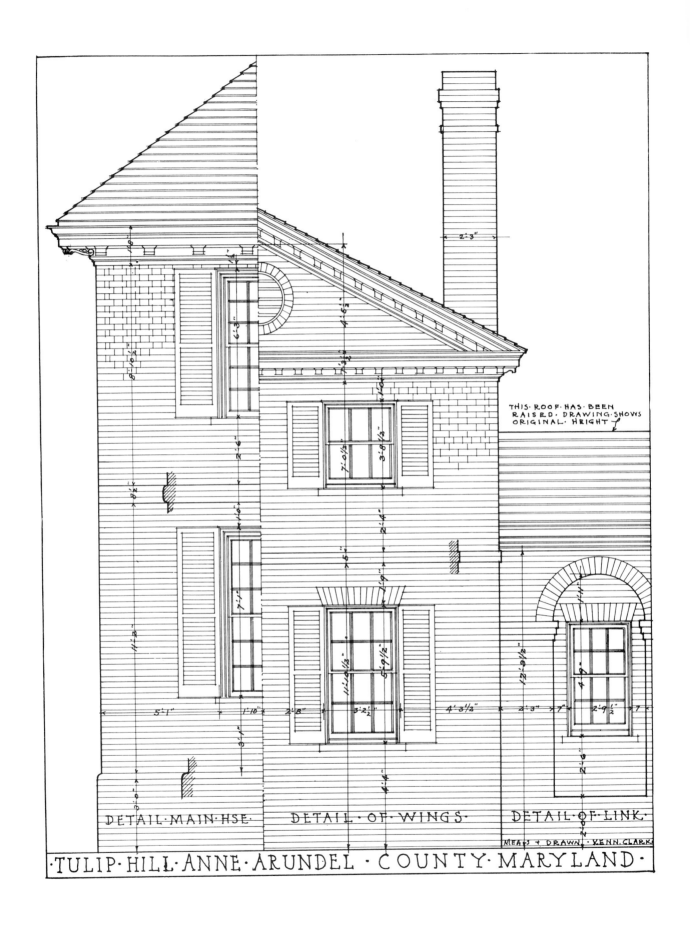

THIS·ROOF·HAS·BEEN
RAISED·DRAWING·SHOWS
ORIGINAL·HEIGHT

·DETAIL·MAIN·HSE·   ·DETAIL·OF·WINGS·   ·DETAIL·OF·LINK·

MEAS + DRAWN KENN.CLARK

·TULIP·HILL·ANNE·ARUNDEL·COUNTY·MARYLAND·

Detail of North Elevation
TULIP HILL, ANNE ARUNDEL COUNTY, MARYLAND

Detail of Wing, South Elevation
TULIP HILL, ANNE ARUNDEL COUNTY, MARYLAND

Detail of Elevation
HOUSE AT MAIN AND CONDUIT STREETS, ANNAPOLIS, MARYLAND

Detail of Drawing Room Mantel
TULIP HILL, ANNE ARUNDEL COUNTY, MARYLAND

Detail of Entrance Hall
TULIP HILL, ANNE ARUNDEL COUNTY, MARYLAND

Entrance Hall

TULIP HILL, ANNE ARUNDEL COUNTY, MARYLAND

SUDLEY, ANNE ARUNDEL COUNTY, MARYLAND

Detail of Stair
TULIP HILL, ANNE ARUNDEL COUNTY, MARYLAND

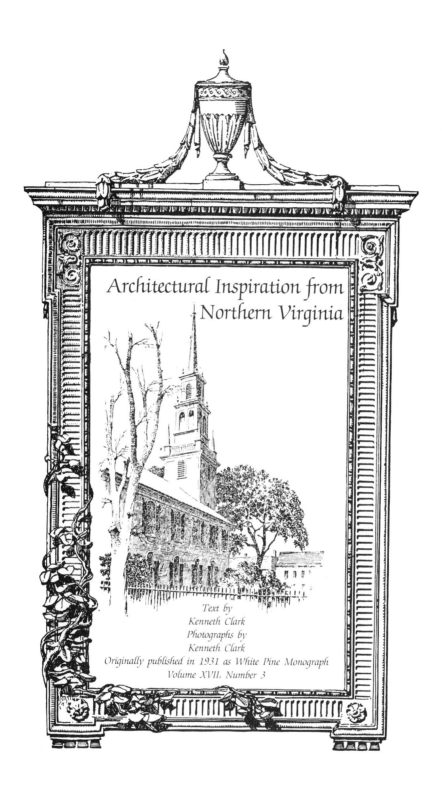

Architectural Inspiration from
Northern Virginia

Text by
Kenneth Clark
Photographs by
Kenneth Clark
Originally published in 1931 as White Pine Monograph
Volume XVII, Number 3

POHICK CHURCH—1769—FAIRFAX COUNTY, VIRGINIA

ARCHITECTURAL INSPIRATION FROM NORTHERN VIRGINIA

DURING the past twelve years, the writer, accompanied by the Editor, has ranged the Eastern Seaboard gathering records of early American architecture in the form of photographs and measured drawings for publication in this series. In such a quest, it would seem that the time would come when it would be increasingly difficult to locate unpublished examples of architectural interest, for when this series was started there was little available data on which to base an estimate of just how much material existed that had the necessary architectural value. After all this time and some one hundred thousand miles of travel, fine examples can still be found in abundance and new fields are constantly being explored which contain worthwhile buildings that are unknown to the profession.

One never ceases to wonder at the quantity of good work done by the early builders in this country; the consistency with which they erected houses, churches, public buildings, that have stood the test of time and through changing conditions of living and public taste have survived to be admired and appreciated by those who study them.

Their variety is infinite and their style ranges from the dignity and sophistication of such Georgian houses as the Hammond House at Annapolis, to the simple, unpretentious farmhouses that cannot be classified, but still have an architectural charm that few modern architects, with all their available source material, equal.

Who created them—who designed them—in the sense that we think of architectural design? Were they architects? Judging from the results, the answer is positively, "Yes," but few, if any, of them boasted of a framed sheepskin or other qualifications that would allow them to call themselves "architects" today. But, nevertheless, they took the requirements of the client and created buildings answering all the requisites of a successfully solved problem. Their houses were livable, their churches dignified and their public buildings practical and over all they worked the spell of beauty of design, of excellence of detail and homogenity of ensemble that today make us wonder if it was all just accident. But, accidents do not happen so often or so consistently.

Undoubtedly, some of those early men were trained; in the majority of cases, self-trained, and only love of a profession can bring a man through that grind to success. Such were Thomas Jefferson, Dr. Thornton and others. But what of those, who, far from large centers where trained men were apt to be, created designs that have lived through changing periods of time, in spite of new conditions and habits and fickle public taste, or lack of it? Their buildings have an innate esthetic value beyond the trammels of a "style." They are perfect solutions of the owners requirements of living and they are beautiful.

Books? Yes, of course, handbooks found their way here from England containing motives for this and that, even complete designs for houses, but we have books too, far and beyond the possession of those early architects. It is only necessary to look about the suburbs to see how our books are sometimes used, or rather misused. During the last few years, however, the standard of design of "Colonial" architecture has undoubtedly taken great strides, due to a broader understanding of the subject. Compare the gimcrack interpretation of the 1890's with the work being done today and this fact is easily recognizable.

Virginia, perhaps with greater claim than any of the early Commonwealths, can be numbered among the first family of Colonies. Its history, full of romantic episodes and famous names, is written large upon the pages of early America. The contributions of this colony to the outstanding architectural examples of the Colonial period are as numerous and significant as any of the original thirteen.

Wealth and prosperity marked its early growth. Huge plantations sprang into being with great manor houses built as residences for the landed proprietors, where they lived in almost regal state, attended by their slaves and servants, carrying on the aristocratic habits and customs to which they and their forefathers were bred in the mother country.

Northern Virginia is particularly rich in these stately mansions. Gunston Hall, illustrated in Volume VIII, Chapter 6, Woodlawn Mansion, Mount Vernon the finest and most complete of any, and others dot the fertile countryside. Many of them have passed from the possession of the families of the original builders and have been purchased by sympathetic admirers whose care of them is well deserved. Others have become historic shrines to be preserved for all time as monuments to famous occupants. Some, indeed many, have disappeared, a sacrifice to time, neglect or disaster.

This chapter comprises a number of buildings and examples of craftsmanship come upon in the course of an exploring trip between Washington, D.C., and Fredericksburg, Virginia.

The first stop was at Falls Church, a town built years after the church from which it took its name. The church has stood, in its picturesque setting, since 1768 when it was built on the site of an earlier structure dating from 1734. The present building has had a romantic history. Washington was elected one of its vestrymen in 1763 and during the Revolution a recruiting station was established in it for the Revolutionary Army. In the chaos of the Civil War days, it was used as a stable for Union calvary horses.

The building is simple and four square like most of the rural Virginia churches. The colorful brick walls are laid in Flemish bond with black headers. The front doorway, of moulded brick, is an excellent example of design and execution.

About ten miles from Falls Church lies old Alexandria, where, in the churchyard of venerable Christ Church, were found the gravestones illustrated. Those of Eleanor and Sarah Wren are of a red stone similar to a fine sandstone. The design and cutting, probably done in England, are particularly fine and the stones are in an excellent state of preservation. The Mumford and Pierce stones are of slate and the lettering was at one time gold leafed. The design and material, as well as the inscriptions, would lead to the belief that they were cut in New England and erected here as memorials to visitors who died and were buried in Alexandria. They are typical of various examples found in New England graveyards.

Woodlawn Mansion stands on a commanding site just off the main highway seven miles south of Alexandria. The land was originally a part of Washington's Mount Vernon estate and was given to Lawrence Lewis, Washington's nephew, on his marriage to Eleanor Parke Custis. The house was designed by Dr. William Thornton, who, tradition says, presented the drawings to the couple as a wedding present.

The house was started in 1801 and finished in 1805. It has passed through many vicissitudes and at one time was falling into ruin. Among its former owners, were Paul and Vaughn Kester and it was here that the latter wrote "The Fortunes of the Landreys." The estate was finally bought by the late Senator Oscar Underwood and is now fully and sympathetically restored and cherished by his widow, to whom we are indebted for the privilege of recording it.

Pohick Church, in Fairfax County, is an historic shrine whose early history is intimately associated with George Washington. From nearby Mount Vernon, he often attended services here. The original church was erected in 1769. The building committee, which consisted of George Washington, George Mason of Gunston Hall, William Fairfax, Daniel McCarthy and Edward Paine, decided in 1764 to replace the wooden building with one of brick. Washington favored a change of site as well and carried his point by producing a map of his own making on which were located the house of each church member and the new site of the church in a more central and accessible position. During the Civil War, the interior was looted by Federal troops and all the woodwork removed. It has been replaced by a modern restoration.

Aquia Church, on Aquia Creek, in Stafford County, was built, according to the inscription over the South door, "in 1757 by Mourning Richards, Undertaker—Wm. Copein Mason." The title "undertaker" in colonial days referred to a contractor and not to a "mortician," though Mr. Richards' first name might indicate otherwise! The walls of Aquia Church are of large size brick laid in Flemish bond, the corners of the building decorated with quoins. The stone of the doorways and trim was quarried near by on Aquia Creek.

The interior is one of the few excellent examples of original woodwork left in the Virginia churches. The "three decker" pulpit with tester, the stall pews, etc., are illustrated on pages 126. The roll of vestrymen of 1757, which is given on a painted wooden tablet on the face of the gallery rail, contains such names as Lee, Fitzhugh, Moncure, Mercer, etc., all of whom were well known in the history of early Virginia. Services are still held here once or twice a month and the building is cared for by the Aquia Association.

The house known as the "Sentry Box" in Fredericksburg, is located on a site that commands a view of the Rappahannock River. Its name is derived from the fact that during three wars—the Revolution, the War of 1812 and the Civil War—it was used as a vantage point to observe the river for the coming of enemy ships or boats. It is known as one of the oldest houses in Fredericksburg.

From Washington to Fredericksburg, via Falls Church, is a distance of approximately seventy miles. All the material illustrated in this chapter, as well as Gunston Hall and Mount Vernon Mansion is in this territory. Mount Vernon, unfortunately, is barred from publication by an edict of the present owners. Few sections of the country can boast of so many inspirational examples of Colonial work in such a limited territory, but Virginia is rich in architectural heritage, the study of which can be of tremendous value in the work of the modern designer who desires to create buildings that will perhaps not have the startling thrill of some modern examples, but will reflect the substantial gentility and artistic appreciation of our forefathers.

AQUIA CHURCH—1757—STAFFORD COUNTY, VIRGINIA

Doorway on West Elevation
AQUIA CHURCH — 1757 — STAFFORD COUNTY, VIRGINIA

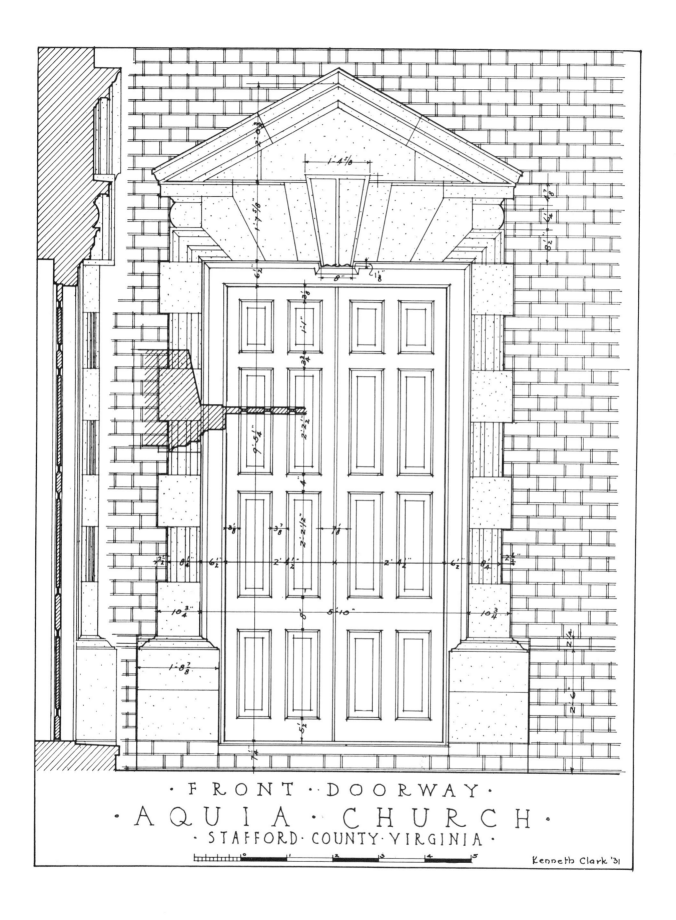

· F R O N T · D O O R W A Y ·
· A Q U I A · C H U R C H ·
· STAFFORD · COUNTY · VIRGINIA ·

Kenneth Clark '31

South Transept Elevation
AQUIA CHURCH — 1757 — STAFFORD COUNTY, VIRGINIA

Doorway on West Elevation
FALLS CHURCH—1768—FAIRFAX COUNTY, VIRGINIA

FALLS CHURCH—1768—FAIRFAX COUNTY, VIRGINIA

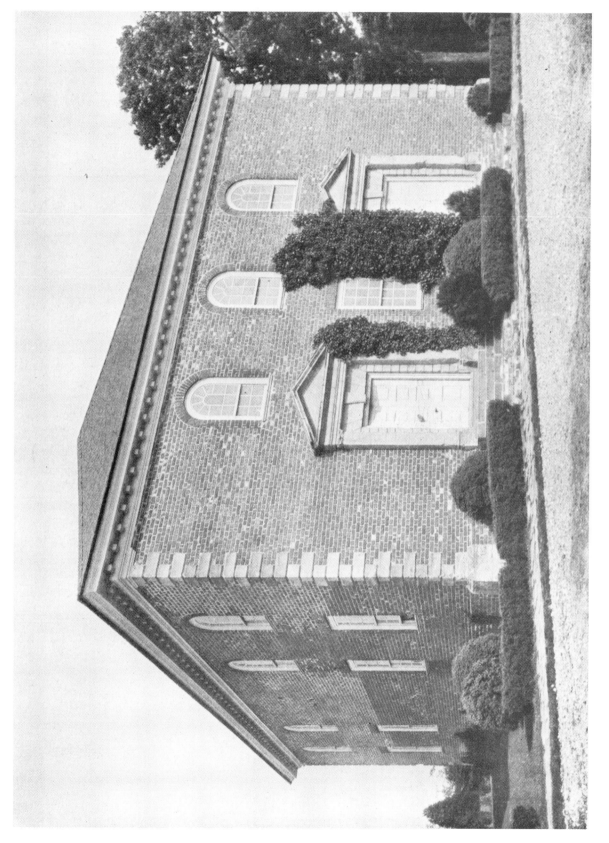

POHICK CHURCH—1769—FAIRFAX COUNTY, VIRGINIA

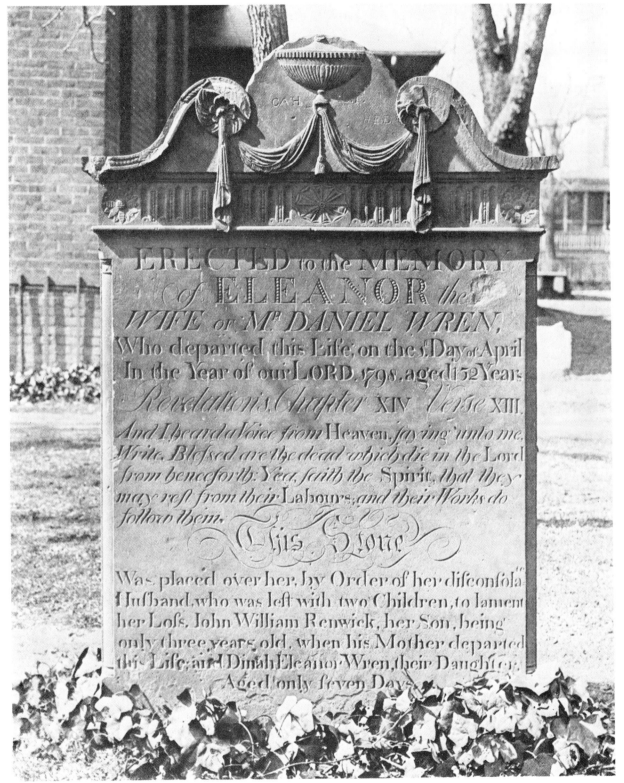

Christ Churchyard
GRAVESTONE OF ELEANOR WREN, ALEXANDRIA, VIRGINIA

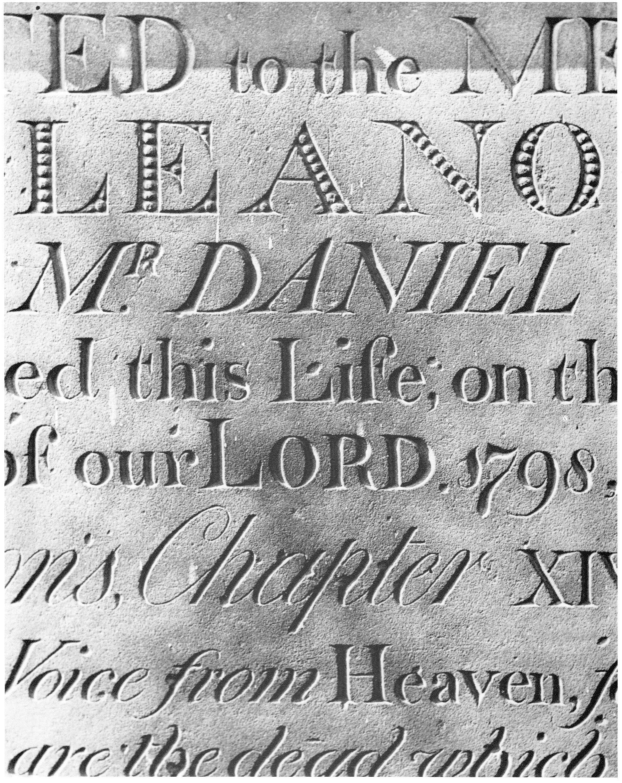

Detail of Lettering
GRAVESTONE OF ELEANOR WREN, ALEXANDRIA, VIRGINIA

Sacred to the Memory
of
Mrs. MARY CRANDELL
the amiable Confort of
Mr. THOMAS CRANDELL
She was born at
Newport, Rhode-Island,
December 20th 1753
and Died the 16th of
January, 1800.

Here lies
Mr ISA
Born in
Mr ISAAC
Who dep
Marc.
Aged

In MEMORY of
Wife of Iohn Wren
Edward Lewis
Aug, 13, 1792th

VARIOUS EXAMPLES OF
LETTERING FROM·DIRECT
RUBBINGS·OF GRAVE-
STONES IN CHRIST
CHURCHYARD AT
ALEXANDRIA·VIRGINIA.

ER
C
WIF
Who d
In the
Rev

he Body of

C PIERCE

ofton. Son of

ERCE, Diftiller.

ed this Life

26th. 1771.

4 Years

This Monument
sacred to the Memory
of the once lov'd & efteem'd
Capt GEORGE MUMFORD
late of NEW LONDON in the
Colony of CONNECTICUT. He
departed this Tranfitory
Life at GEORGE TOWN July 7th
1773. in the 28th year of his age

CTED to the MEMORY

ELEANOR the

of MR DANIEL WREN,

parted this Life, on the 5ft Day of April

ear of our LORD. 1798, aged 32 Years

tions, Chapter XIV Verse XIII.

DRAWN·FROM·RUBBINGS·BY·KENNETH·CLARK·

SEE DETAIL OF LETTERING ON PAGE 119

Gravestones—CHRIST CHURCHYARD, ALEXANDRIA, VIRGINIA

THE OLDEST STONE NOW STANDING

Detail of Lettering

GRAVESTONE OF SARAH WREN, CHRIST CHURCHYARD, ALEXANDRIA, VIRGINIA

West Elevation

WOODLAWN MANSION, FAIRFAX COUNTY, VIRGINIA

East Elevation

WOODLAWN MANSION, FAIRFAX COUNTY, VIRGINIA

Detail of East Elevation
WOODLAWN MANSION, FAIRFAX COUNTY, VIRGINIA

Detail of East Elevation
WOODLAWN MANSION, FAIRFAX COUNTY, VIRGINIA

Hall and Stairway
WOODLAWN MANSION, FAIRFAX COUNTY, VIRGINIA

Mantel in Drawing Room
WOODLAWN MANSION, FAIRFAX COUNTY, VIRGINIA

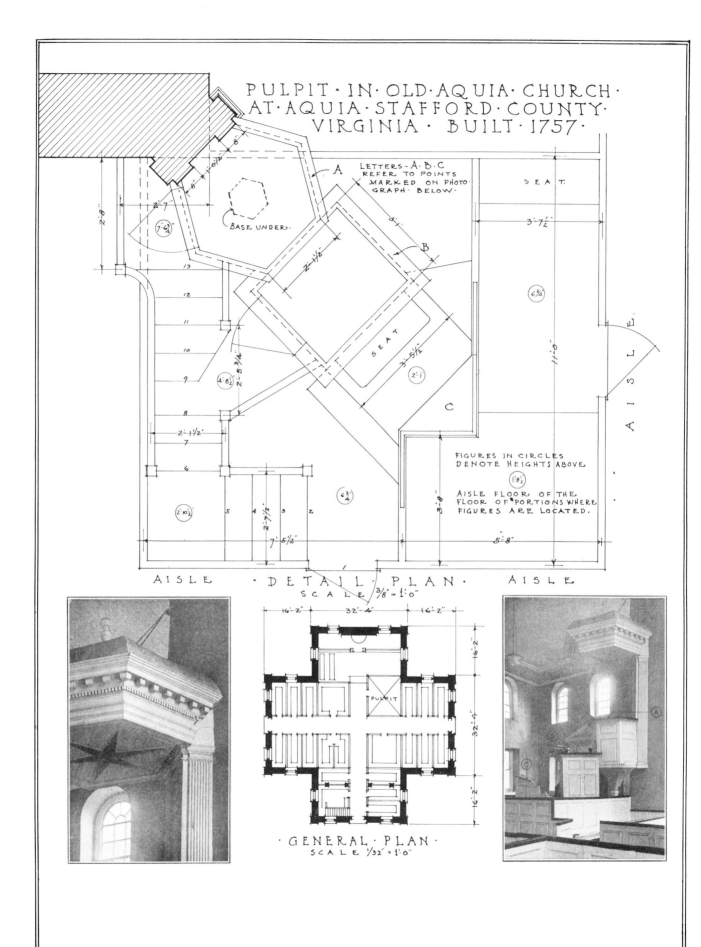

PULPIT · IN · OLD · AQUIA · CHURCH ·
AT · AQUIA · STAFFORD · COUNTY ·
VIRGINIA · BUILT · 1757 ·

LETTERS · A · B · C
REFER · TO · POINTS
MARKED · ON · PHOTO
GRAPH · BELOW.

A

BASE UNDER.

B

SEAT

SEAT

C

SEAT

FIGURES IN CIRCLES
DENOTE HEIGHTS ABOVE

AISLE FLOOR OF THE
FLOOR OF PORTIONS WHERE
FIGURES ARE LOCATED.

AISLE   · DETAIL · PLAN ·   AISLE
SCALE 3/8" = 1:0"

· GENERAL · PLAN ·
SCALE 1/32" = 1:0"

PULPIT

"SENTRY BOX," FREDERICKSBURG, VIRGINIA

MARY WASHINGTON HOUSE, FREDERICKSBURG, VIRGINIA

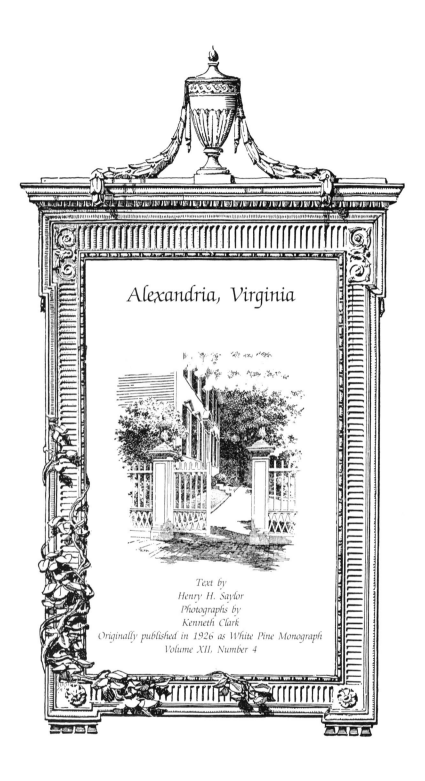

Alexandria, Virginia

Text by
Henry H. Saylor
Photographs by
Kenneth Clark
Originally published in 1926 as White Pine Monograph
Volume XII, Number 4

Entrance Detail
FAIRFAX HOUSE, ALEXANDRIA, VIRGINIA

ALEXANDRIA, VIRGINIA

ALEXANDRIA, like several other early settlements in America, might have been, but for a whim of Fate, one of the great ports of the Atlantic seaboard. The tide of immigration to the new continent touched the cove that nestled here under the Potomac's high banks, eddied about it for a time, and then swept on to make a Baltimore.

In July, 1608, Captain John Smith and fourteen companions imbued with some of his own intrepid spirit of exploration, sailed up the Potomac River and were the first white men to look upon the site of what was to become Alexandria. They saw merely a small encampment of Doeg Indians, a tribe of the Algonquins, who were friendly and hospitable.

By 1631 there had gathered in the neighborhood a few settlers, who built a tobacco storehouse and called the hamlet Belle Haven. In 1669 Robert Howison obtained a patent for land upon which the little cove settlement was situated, but instead of taking it up, sold the patent to John Alexander, a Stafford planter, for the consideration of 6000 pounds of tobacco. Not until 1695 was there a settlement upon the grant under the patent, when Thomas Pearson sailed up the river and located upon Pearson's Island, and it was over half a century later, in 1749, that William Ramsay, John Carlyle and associates founded Alexandria.

On March 9, 1780, a government was set up, Alexandria being then over thirty years old. The town spread itself upon a high plateau, extending from Oronoco Creek and its marsh on the north and northwest, to the river shore on the east, and to what was known as the White Oak Swamp on the southwest and south.

It was a town marked by deep loyalty to the Crown, if we may judge by the names given its streets. Royal and Fairfax were the two long streets, crossed by Cameron, King, Queen, Prince, Princess, Duke and Duchess. These shorter cross streets, cutting through to reach the cove below, rounded off the sharp edge of the bluff which had long formed the line of demarcation between the cove and the high plateau. Later on, when loyalty to the King gave place to national self-consciousness, the streets reflected no less definitely the heroes of the new republic, in Wolfe, Wilkes, Pitt, St. Asaph and Patrick Henry, for whom a double measure of pride was expressed in the naming of two streets.

Tobacco was the chief product of the surrounding countryside, and there is probably not an acre within the town limits that has not produced its hundredweight of good Oronoco. With a good harbor and the ability to produce something that the outside world wanted, Alexandria grew rapidly as a trading port for foreign commerce.

Then came the event that proved to be the turning point in the town's march of progress. In August, 1814, two British frigates sailed up the river and took the town. Fort Warburton, designed to protect the community from such an attack, had just been depleted by a withdrawal of troops, and the officer in charge, feeling that resistance would be futile, blew up his arsenal and abandoned the fort. The invaders looted the town, carrying off quantities of tobacco and grains stored in the port warehouses, and Alexandria's commercial activities suffered a blow from which they never fully recovered. Meanwhile, her rival port, Baltimore, forged ahead, and Alexandria's promised greatness became merely something that might have been. To complete the wreck of great hopes, a fire swept the town in 1827, burning fifty-three houses.

Alexandria's loss, however, is perhaps the gain of architectural students and antiquarians today, for in the little town the march of progress has not swept aside so much of the simple, lovingly detailed work of the late eighteenth century and the early years of the nineteenth as in other places where the work of these years has so largely been destroyed in the making of what were fondly thought to be improvements.

Most widely known among the buildings that still remain, wholly or in part, are three that have unusual significance, not only architecturally but as settings for historical events in the early days of the republic. These are Christ Church, the Carlyle House and Gadsby's Tavern. No student of the early architecture of America thinks of Alexandria, Virginia, apart from these three great landmarks; they *are* Alexandria, but, as some of the photographs reproduced in this monograph show, there are other bits that should not be lost to architectural history—a cornice here, an entrance doorway there, a naive bit of wood construction. It is with this thought in mind that the present selection of material is brought together, stressing less the better known work, which has appeared from time to time elsewhere, than some minor details that might otherwise be overlooked and soon pass into oblivion.

Nevertheless, the background of all this work, the flavor of Alexandria, can best be conveyed as relating to her three great landmarks. They, of course, rather than any minor building or unrelated detail, bring to a focus those faraway days on the Potomac—their intensity, the resolute single-mindedness of the men who made them epochal, the innate dignity and taste of their unsophistication, the craftsmanship that so evidently found real joy in itself.

Christ Church, Alexandria, scarcely less than Pohick Church itself, bears an aura of close association with George Washington. He was a vestryman of both churches—his father, Augustine Washington, had been a vestryman of Truro Parish before him—and when Christ Church was opened for worship, purchased his pew for the sum of £26:10:8. Tradition has it that both he and Thomas Jefferson had a hand in the design of Christ Church, though it seems more likely that the building was chiefly the work of James Wren, said to have been a descendent of Sir Christopher.

The church was started about 1765, the contract for its erection being awarded to James Parsons for £600. But, like many of the early churches, it was long in the building, being finished only in 1773 after Parsons had given up the task and Col. John Carlyle had undertaken, in 1772, to complete it for the additional sum of £220. On February 27, 1773, it was finally completed in its original form and dedicated. The gallery was added about 1800 and the tower somewhat later. In design, Christ Church bears a strong resemblance to the later and perhaps better known Pohick Church, differing chiefly in the tower that was added later and a pedimented Palladian window at the opposite end. This similarity of design is not surprising, considering the fact that George Washington himself made the drawings for Pohick Church, and, being a vestryman of Christ Church at the time, had access to Wren's drawings for the earlier building.

It was on the green in front of Christ Church that George Washington, talking earnestly with a few of his friends and neighbors of the tea thrown overboard in Boston Harbor, definitely committed himself to the policy of resistance—and the birth of a new nation became imminent.

A hundred years later, upon the same church green, on a Sabbath morning in May, a retired soldier stood talking with his friends and neighbors. Besought by all, Robert E. Lee here tacitly accepted the command of the Armies of the Commonwealth.

The Carlyle House, second of Alexandria's hallowed landmarks, lately a part of the Braddock Hotel on Fairfax Street, was built by John Carlyle in 1745, upon the foundations of what had been an old stone fort, erected possibly as early as 1638. Carlyle was a prosperous merchant, as may be surmised from the fact that he built this mansion when but twenty-five years old.

Colonel John Carlyle, a close friend of George Washington's, who had married one of the Fairfax family, made his home a center of the social and political life of the day. Here we find gathered such figures in the nation's history as Thomas Jefferson, Aaron Burr, John Marshall, Charles Carroll, John Paul Jones, and James Rumsey, inventor of the first steamboat.

Gadsby's Tavern, third of the architectural monuments by which Alexandria is known, was one of the great stopping places between north and south in the days when stage coaches rumbled over the King's Highway. Originally called Claggett's Tavern, it was built by John Wise in 1792, and few travelers from Williamsburg, Richmond and the south passed by it on their way to Philadelphia without partaking of its widely famous hospitality. Here in the great ballroom, which is now forever preserved against disintegration in the American Wing of the Metropolitan Museum of Art, were held the famous Birthnight Balls, in honor of the King and Queen. And here, growing out of that early custom, was instituted in 1798 the first public celebration of Washington's Birthday, with the beloved General himself present.

Lafayette was an honored guest at Gadsby's in 1824 —his second visit to Alexandria, for in 1777 he passed through the town on his way to join Washington's army.

Today Alexandria, like Williamsburg, turns her thoughts back to the great days of old. What can a mere future offer to the town which was George Washington's post office, his place of voting? Here he had his surveyor's office, here brought for sale the produce of his farms. It was here he came to attend Masonic Lodge. Into Alexandria's streets often rolled the coach from Mount Vernon, bringing the family to some social gathering at Colonel Carlyle's or to a dance at Gadsby's Tavern. Here dwelt Dr. Laurie, who attended all Washington's people by contract at £15 the year; Dr. Craik and Dr. Elisha Dick, both of whom attended the General in his last illness. It was from Alexandria that Washington as the young surveyor had set out upon his Western expeditions, and, later, to fight in the wars with the French. He represented the town in the House of Burgesses, surveyed its streets, was a member of its Town Council, and here, on the steps of Gadsby's, the General held his last military review.

Alexandria looks backward, proud of her glorious past, and we, standing afar off, would share her pride, for what was hers is now the heritage of all of us.

CHRIST CHURCH, ALEXANDRIA, VIRGINIA

LEE AND BURSON HOUSES, ORONOCO STREET, ALEXANDRIA, VIRGINIA

HOUSE AT NUMBER 711 PRINCE STREET, ALEXANDRIA, VIRGINIA

Entrance Detail
HOUSE AT NUMBER 711 PRINCE STREET, ALEXANDRIA, VIRGINIA

FAIRFAX HOUSE, CAMERON STREET, ALEXANDRIA, VIRGINIA

Entrance Detail
OLD CITY TAVERN, ALEXANDRIA, VIRGINIA

Central Portion of Front Elevation
COLROSS HOUSE ALEXANDRIA, VIRGINIA

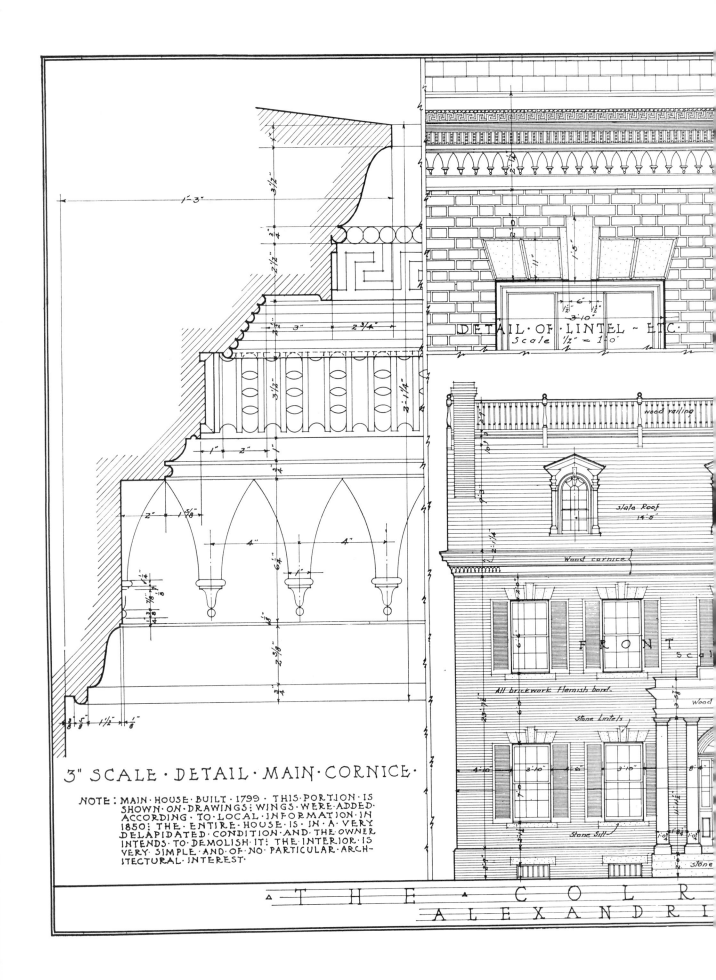

DETAIL·OF·LINTEL~ETC.
Scale 1/2" = 1'·0"

3" SCALE · DETAIL · MAIN · CORNICE ·

NOTE: MAIN·HOUSE·BUILT·1799· THIS·PORTION·IS
SHOWN·ON·DRAWINGS; WINGS·WERE·ADDED·
ACCORDING·TO·LOCAL·INFORMATION·IN
1850; THE·ENTIRE·HOUSE·IS·IN·A·VERY·
DELAPIDATED·CONDITION·AND·THE·OWNER
INTENDS·TO·DEMOLISH·IT; THE·INTERIOR·IS
VERY·SIMPLE·AND·OF·NO·PARTICULAR·ARCH-
ISTECTURAL·INTEREST.

FRONT

Slate Roof
14'·5"

Wood cornice

Wood railing

All brickwork Flemish bond.

Stone Lintels

Stone Sill

△ · T H E · C O L R
A L E X A N D R I

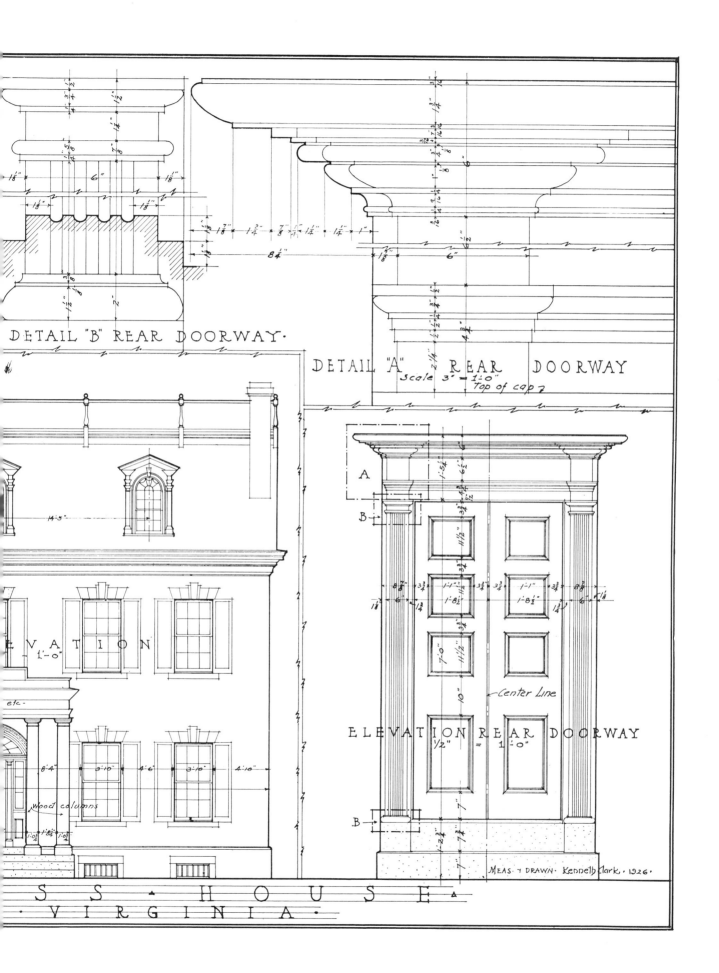

DETAIL "B" REAR DOORWAY.

DETAIL "A" REAR DOORWAY
Scale 3" = 1'-0"
Top of cap

A

B

ELEVATION
1'-0"

etc.

Wood columns

E L E V A T I O N R E A R D O O R W A Y
1/2" = 1'-0"

Center Line

B

MEAS. & DRAWN. Kenneth Clark. 1926.

· S S · H O U S E ·
· V I R G I N I A ·

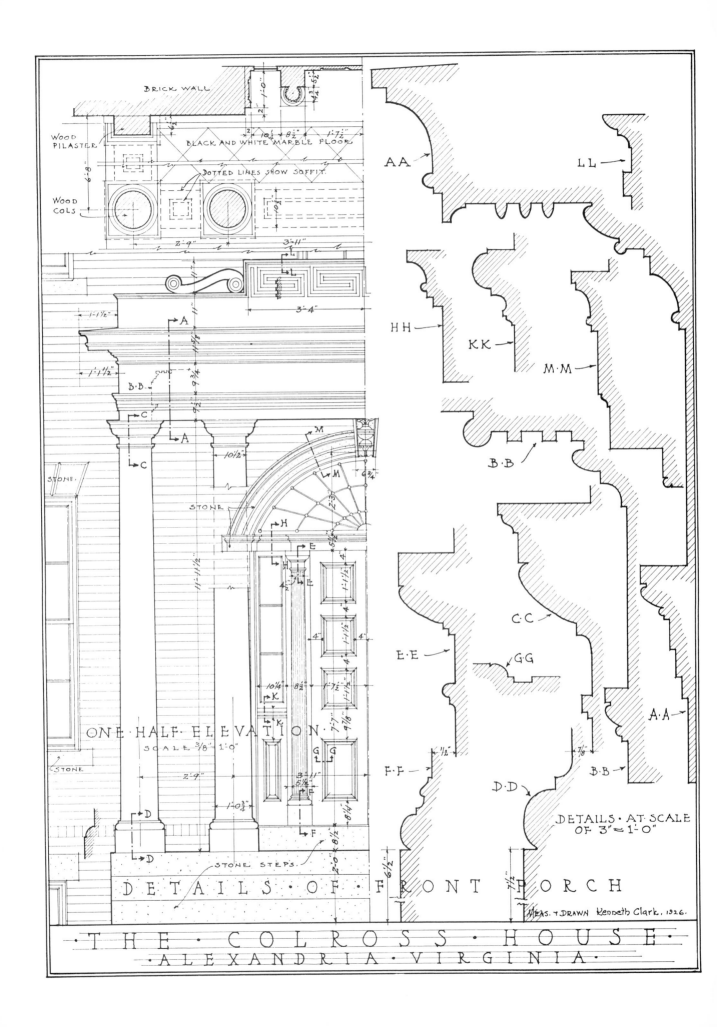

BRICK WALL

WOOD PILASTER

BLACK AND WHITE MARBLE FLOOR

WOOD COLS

DOTTED LINES SHOW SOFFIT.

2'-9"

3'-11"

3'-4"

STONE

A

B·B

C

A

STONE

C

STONE

M

M

STONE

H

E

E

K

K

G G

ONE·HALF·ELEVATION·
SCALE 3/8"=1'-0"

2'-9"

1'-0¾"

D

D

STONE STEPS.

F

F

DETAILS·OF·FRONT·PORCH

AA

LL

HH

KK

MM

B·B

C·C

G·G

E·E

A·A

F·F

D·D

B·B

DETAILS·AT·SCALE
OF 3"=1'-0"

MEAS.+DRAWN Kenneth Clark. 1926.

·THE·COLROSS·HOUSE·
·ALEXANDRIA·VIRGINIA·

Rear Doorway

Main Cornice
COLROSS HOUSE, ALEXANDRIA, VIRGINIA

"LIGHT HORSE" HARRY LEE HOUSE AND 609 CAMERON STREET, ALEXANDRIA, VIRGINIA

HOUSE AT NUMBER 711 PRINCESS STREET, ALEXANDRIA, VIRGINIA

Doorway Detail
HOUSE AT 711 PRINCESS STREET, ALEXANDRIA, VIRGINIA

LLOYD HOUSE, WASHINGTON STREET, ALEXANDRIA, VIRGINIA

Detail of Dormer Window
COLROSS HOUSE, ALEXANDRIA, VIRGINIA

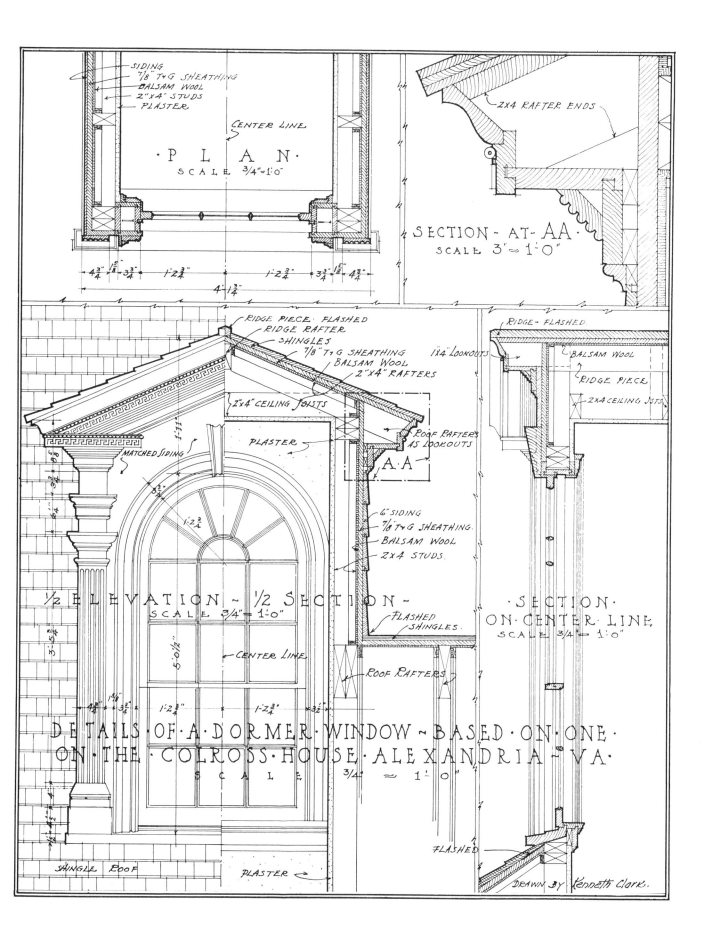

SIDING
7/8" T+G SHEATHING
BALSAM WOOL
2"×4" STUDS
PLASTER

CENTER LINE

·P L A N·
SCALE 3/4"=1'0"

2×4 RAFTER ENDS

SECTION·AT·AA·
SCALE 3"=1'0"

RIDGE PIECE FLASHED
RIDGE RAFTER
SHINGLES
7/8" T+G SHEATHING
BALSAM WOOL
2"×4" RAFTERS

RIDGE·FLASHED

BALSAM WOOL

RIDGE PIECE

1×4 LOOKOUTS

2×4 CEILING JSTS

2"×4" CEILING JOISTS

PLASTER

ROOF RAFTERS AS LOOKOUTS

A A

MATCHED SIDING

6" SIDING
7/8" T+G SHEATHING
BALSAM WOOL
2×4 STUDS

1/2 ELEVATION ~ 1/2 SECTION·
SCALE 3/4" = 1'0"

·SECTION·
ON·CENTER·LINE·
SCALE 3/4" = 1'0"

FLASHED SHINGLES

CENTER LINE

ROOF RAFTERS

DETAILS·OF·A·DORMER·WINDOW ~ BASED·ON·ONE
ON·THE·COLROSS·HOUSE·ALEXANDRIA ~ VA·
SCALE   3/4" = 1'0"

SHINGLE ROOF

PLASTER

FLASHED

DRAWN BY Kenneth Clark.

HOUSE ON CORNER OF FAIRFAX AND WOLFE STREETS, ALEXANDRIA, VIRGINIA

Old Salem, North Carolina

Text by
Hall Crews
Photographs by
Kenneth Clark
Originally published in 1929 as White Pine Monograph
Volume XV, Number 2

CUPOLA OF HOME MORAVIAN CHURCH FROM REAR OF OLD SALEM BOYS' SCHOOL,
(SALEM) WINSTON-SALEM, NORTH CAROLINA

OLD SALEM, NORTH CAROLINA

WHAT a request! That of Mr. Russell White-head to the writer; that I write a chapter on the old buildings of Salem, North Carolina. Almost any one of the old structures selected for illustration would form subject matter for a chapter and of this beautiful old town, with its marvelous background, much could be written.

Who settled this old town? Empire Builders! Let us take a tiny peep into the distant past for an historical background, and we will see a pageantry of war and persecution.

Attilla and his Huns destroying Bohemia about 800 A.D. Prince Mojmir building churches in Moravia, a province of Bohemia, in 836 A.D. John Huss, who was born in Bohemia in 1369. Gregory, the Patriarch. Formation of Unitas Fratrum, *The United Brethren*, now the Moravian Church, in 1457. Luke of Prague, born in 1460. Martin Luther! John Augusta, son of a hatter, born in Prague in 1500. The Brethren driven from Bohemia and Moravia. John Amos Commenius and Christan David, who led the Brethren to a refuge on the great wooded estate of Count Nicholas Louis von Zinzendorf located in Hurrnhut, Saxony. Under the patronage of Count Zinzendorf, we see their movement into Germany 1735–1775 and into England 1728–1775 and to America; their arrival in Georgia, under the leadership of Spangenberg, in 1735 and their movement to Pennsylvania 1740–1775.

Spangenberg, with a small band of men, left Bethlehem, Pennsylvania, November 29th, 1751 and located, in North Carolina, a tract of 100,000 acres granted the brethren by Lord Granville. Spangenberg completed his survey January 25th, 1753 and named the tract Wachovia. On October 8th, 1753, twelve single brethren set out from Bethlehem for Wachovia. This small group of men included a pastor, warden, physician, tailor, baker, shoemaker, tanner, gardener and three farmers. They arrived on November 17th, to start the building of Bethabra known to us as Old Town. About the Old Town church was constructed a fort to which, later on, came many other settlers for protection from Indians. The old fort has disappeared but a quiet little path still leads to God's Acre, or the burying ground, with its quaintly lettered soapstone markers, where rest many of these early Empire Builders. In 1756, the colony of Bethabra consisted of sixty-five souls.

It had always been the intention of these first settlers to establish a town near the center of their tract where greater activities could be undertaken. On February 14th, 1765, a site, eight miles south of Bethabra, was chosen and christened Salem by Count Zinzendorf.

Frederick William von Marshall took a very active part in the selection of the site. His resting place can be seen in the present awe inspiring God's Acre of Salem, the simple flat stone bearing the dates 1721–1802.

Only a few years ago Salem was united with Winston and together they form the city of Winston-Salem.

But I wander from my real purpose. I was requested to write of the buildings of these hardy souls and not their history. So to some of their accomplishments!

The Church at Bethabra was erected in 1788, the first Church of Wachovia. The charm of this building lies in simple design, rugged masonry, stone and wide pine plank floors, wide pine plank ceilings, simple detail and inspiring cupola. Truly, its designer was an artist! I wish the reader could see its barrel vaulted cellar, its roof framing connected with pins and the ingenuous method of supporting its cupola.

The Home Moravian Church of Salem page 156 erected in 1800, is, like the Old Town Church, characterized by its beautiful stone and brick masonry, wonderful joinery, simple design and general dignity. The interior has been rebuilt, the plan having been reversed and enlarged.

From the large stone platform in front of the entrance, on every Easter morning, before the sun has risen, the Venerable Bishop speaks a few simple words to the assembled multitude and the slow and solemn march starts on its journey of a few hundred yards to God's Acre, to the music of carols, accompanied by a band of several hundred instruments. Here the Bishop completes the simple service as the sun rises!

The Sisters House was erected in two units, the two doorways of the left being in the first unit. The point where the second unit was added is easily distinguished.

The cornerstone of the first unit was laid on March 31st, 1785 and was dedicated April 5th, 1786. For many years this building was the center of Women's Activities in the community.

This old masterpiece is rich in its lovely crown of orange roof tile blended with black; its European suggestion in fenestration and dormers, brick masonry, hand wrought hardware, simple and dignified detail, perfect proportion, old whitewashed plaster and wide plank and stone floors scrubbed clean.

The Brothers House, like the Sisters House, was erected in two units. The frame structure on the right was begun August 30th 1768 and was dedicated December 27th, 1769. The brick addition to the left was added in 1786. The Brothers House was for many years the industrial center of the community. The street level in front of this building was originally much lower than at present, thus permitting cellar windows.

The construction of the frame unit of this building is unusual. Logs of large diameter being difficult to secure, without transporting them seven or eight miles,

CHURCH AT BETHABRA, NOW KNOWN AS OLD TOWN, NORTH CAROLINA

The outside walls, above grade, are constructed of extremely large handmade clay brick, 11⅞″ x 5″ x 2¾″, laid Flemish bond. We in modern times in laying up a wall of this character in Flemish bond would cut a brick to form a "closer" to fill the rectangle at the corners of alternate courses; not so these people. They molded and burned tiny clay bricks to fill these voids.

The present Office Building, Salem College, was erected in 1810 and was used as the residence of the first "Inspector" of Salem Female Academy. It carries an echo of the detail of the Sisters House. A stone vaulted cellar is an interesting feature. The entrance detail is shown on page 159.

which was a long distance in those days, the walls of this building were constructed of logs of smaller diameter, erected *vertically* in two or more layers having their interstices filled with clay mixed with straw. The interior side of the walls was plastered; the exterior surfaces being covered with "clapboards," as we know them. This makes me think that possibly those who contend that this early outside covering was really known as "clayboards" are correct.

The Vogler House was erected in 1819 by John Vogler, a silversmith and expert cabinet-maker. The building, formerly his shop, shows at the left on page 167.

The entrance to the house is a gem. It is seen on pages

HOME MORAVIAN CHURCH—1800—(SALEM) WINSTON-SALEM, NORTH CAROLINA

CHURCH AT BETHABRA—OLD TOWN (1788)

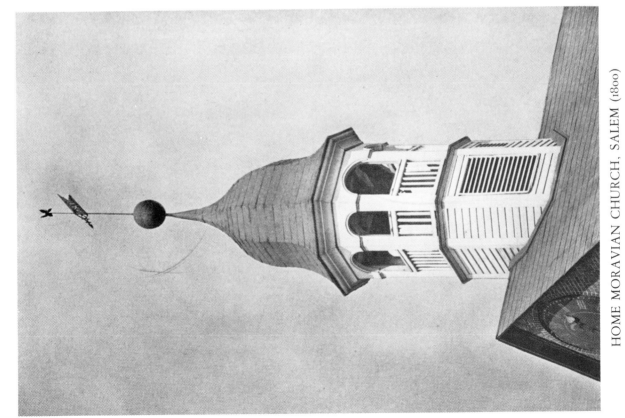

HOME MORAVIAN CHURCH, SALEM (1800)

CUPOLA DETAILS OF TWO MORAVIAN CHURCHES, (SALEM) WINSTON-SALEM, NORTH CAROLINA

WACHOVIA HISTORICAL SOCIETY BUILDING, (SALEM) WINSTON-SALEM, NORTH CAROLINA
Formerly the Salem Boys School, Erected 1794

162–167. The interesting details are further shown by measured drawings in Kenneth Clark's own inimitable style.

The Salem Boys School was organized in 1777. The school building was begun May 1st, 1794 and occupied until 1896. It now shelters the collections of the Wachovia Historical Society.

In this old building, the first story walls are of stone,

her sisters as a residence-studio. Its quaint and dignified interior is a place where one may visit and reminisce.

A detail of the staircase is shown on page 172. It is interesting to note that the bandsawn balustrade with its simple handrail is typical of the staircases in both the Old Town Church and the Salem Boys' School.

The Bishop's House (page 170) was erected in 1841 by the Moravians as a place of residence for the Bishop of

Residence of First Inspector, Salem Female Academy, Now Office Building
SALEM COLLEGE, WINSTON-SALEM, NORTH CAROLINA

stuccoed, its details are similar to the Sisters House, an old oven and vaulting add interest to its interior. The principal feature of the interior is a continuous winding staircase, three stories in height, with details similar to the staircase in the Tavern (page 172).

The site for the Old Salem Tavern was selected in 1768. The first building was destroyed by fire January 31st, 1784. The present building (page 171) was erected during the same year. General George Washington was entertained in this hostelry May 31st, 1791.

The building has been sympathetically restored by Miss Ada Allen and is now occupied by Miss Allen and

the Southern Province. Though of later date, it bears a striking resemblance in proportion, design and detail to those buildings already described.

All of Salem's ancient buildings are characterized by their simplicity and remarkable craftsmanship. Surely their builders must have been inspired. Nothing was wasted; everything was adequate.

These early builders founded an individual community which has grown to be a great city in a great state. We who know and love their purposes, ideals and hardships look upon their aesthetic accomplishments with awe!

Detail of Entrance to Present Office Building
SALEM COLLEGE–1810–(SALEM) WINSTON-SALEM, NORTH CAROLINA

ENTRANCE TO BROTHERS HOUSE, ERECTED 1768–1769

ENTRANCE TO SISTERS HOUSE, ERECTED 1785–1786

Doorway Details—MORAVIAN BUILDINGS, (SALEM) WINSTON-SALEM, NORTH CAROLINA

MORAVIAN BROTHERS HOUSE, (SALEM) WINSTON-SALEM, NORTH CAROLINA

JOHN VOGLER HOUSE — 1819 — (SALEM) WINSTON-SALEM, NORTH CAROLINA

Detail Showing Entrance Hood
JOHN VOGLER HOUSE, (OLD SALEM) WINSTON-SALEM, NORTH CAROLINA

SHINGLE ROOF

MATCHED BOARDS

GLASS

GLASS

"DUTCH" DOOR

PRESENT GRADE

· SECTION ·   ⅜" SCALE · DETAIL · OF · CENTRAL · PART · OF · FRONT

· THE · JOHN · V

· WINSTON · SALEM

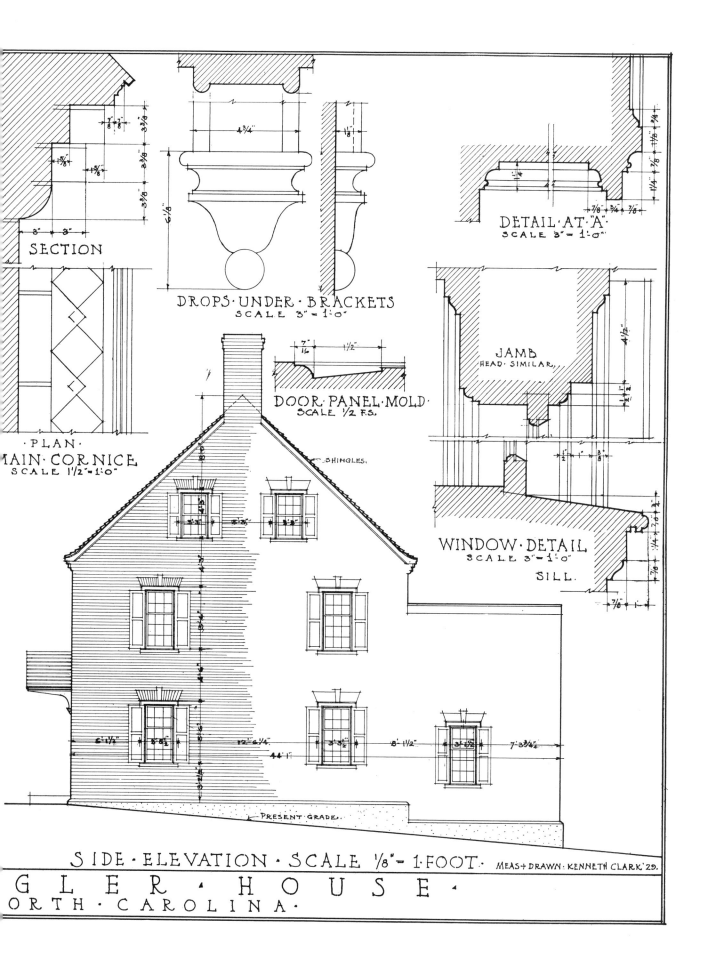

SECTION

DROPS·UNDER·BRACKETS
SCALE 3"=1'-0"

DETAIL·AT·"A"
SCALE 3"=1'-0"

·PLAN·
MAIN·CORNICE
SCALE 1½"=1'-0"

DOOR·PANEL·MOLD
SCALE ½ F.S.

JAMB
HEAD·SIMILAR

WINDOW·DETAIL
SCALE 3"=1'-0"

SILL·

SHINGLES.

PRESENT·GRADE.

SIDE·ELEVATION·SCALE ⅛"= 1·FOOT· MEAS+DRAWN: KENNETH CLARK '29.

GLER·HOUSE·
ORTH·CAROLINA·

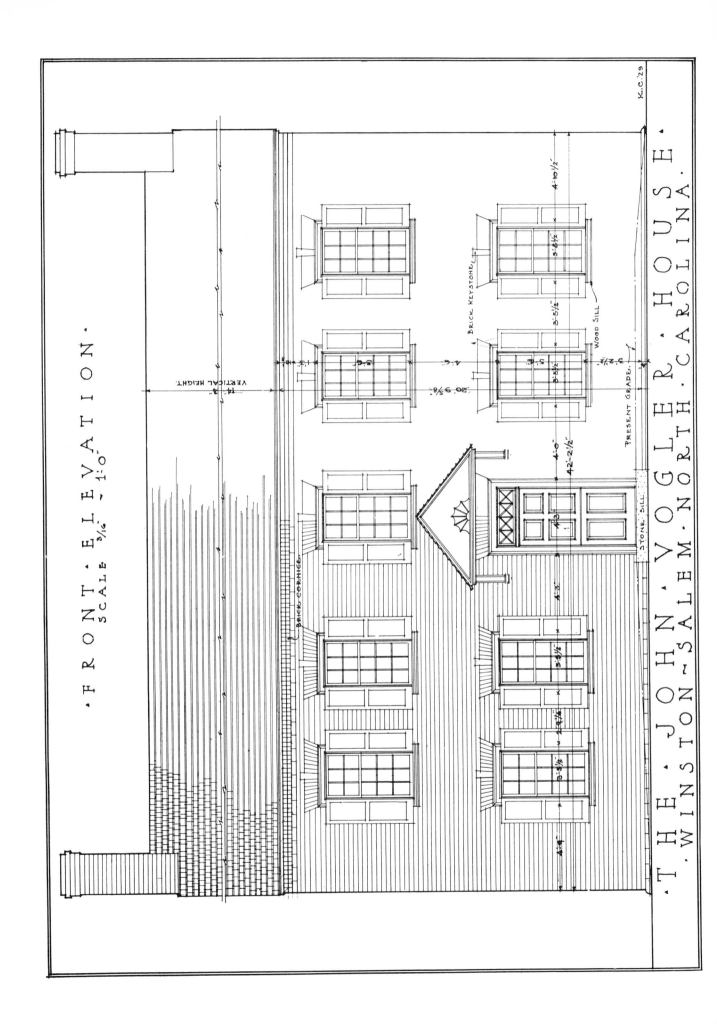

· F R O N T · E L E V A T I O N ·

SCALE 3/16" = 1'-0"

· T H E · J O H N · V O G L E R · H O U S E ·

· W I N S T O N ~ S A L E M · N O R T H · C A R O L I N A ·

K.C. '29

JOHN VOGLER HOUSE—1819—(SALEM) WINSTON-SALEM, NORTH CAROLINA

BROTHERS HOUSE, ERECTED 1768–1769

SISTERS HOUSE, ERECTED 1785–1786

Window Details—MORAVIAN BUILDINGS, (SALEM) WINSTON-SALEM, NORTH CAROLINA

MORAVIAN SISTERS HOUSE — 1785–1786 — (SALEM) WINSTON-SALEM, NORTH CAROLINA

BISHOP'S HOUSE — 1841 — (SALEM) WINSTON-SALEM, NORTH CAROLINA

OLD SALEM TAVERN—1784—(SALEM) WINSTON-SALEM, NORTH CAROLINA

Detail of Staircase
OLD SALEM TAVERN—1784—(SALEM) WINSTON-SALEM, NORTH CAROLINIA

Entrance Detail
HOME MORAVIAN CHURCH — 1800 — WINSTON-SALEM, NORTH CAROLINA

Looking from South Main Street to Church Street
ACADEMY STREET, (SALEM) WINSTON-SALEM, NORTH CAROLINA

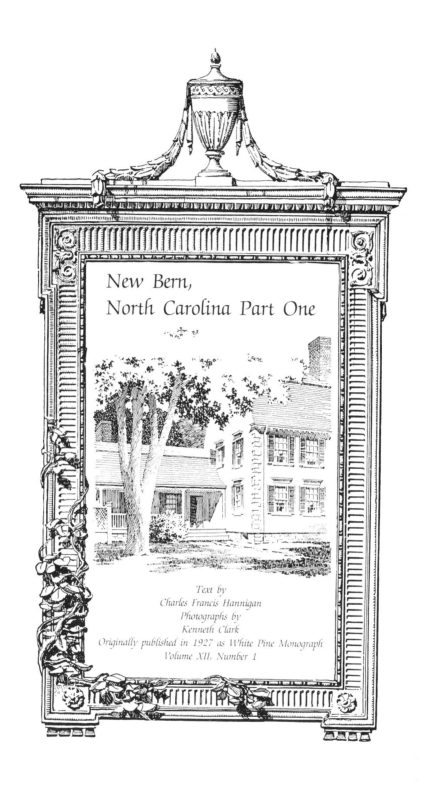

New Bern, North Carolina Part One

Text by
Charles Francis Hannigan
Photographs by
Kenneth Clark
Originally published in 1927 as White Pine Monograph
Volume XII, Number 1

GROENENDYKE (HARGETT) HOUSE, BURN STREET, NEW BERN, NORTH CAROLINA

NEW BERN:
"THE ATHENS OF NORTH CAROLINA"

I DOUBT whether the expert or the amateur alike, will find more and finer expressions of colonial architecture than are so happily presented in this ancient and well preserved seat of England's rule in North America. Here in New Bern, I dare say, the learned and artistic-minded Colonials were as charmed in their day, as we are now, with the sense of beauty nature has so lavishly distilled in eastern North Carolina. The superb trees and flowering shrubbery; the trumpeting loveliness of the landside; the broad, broad rivers; the semitropical climate; impelled them to have their houses stand unashamed in the midst of all this luxury.

Such environment and, maybe, too, the presence in New Bern of the "most beautiful residence in the Americas," the Royal Governor Tryon's palace, challenged their sense of proportion and architectural harmony. Anyhow, you can come to our romantic New Bern and find that what is here imaged forth is but a pallid picture of what rests yet untold.

New Bern, which was once called "Chattawka," is situated on a tongue of land between the Neuse and Trent rivers. The land was purchased from the Indian King Taylor by De Graffenried about 1710, when he joined the Swiss colonists who had embarked in Holland, sailed to northeast England and then for Carolina by way of Virginia.

In 1713 the settlement was broken up by Tuscarora Indians, but by November 1723 we find New Bern made a township covering two hundred and fifty acres and soon after it became the capital of the colony. It was the second town in North Carolina, Bath having been laid out in 1705. In the second year of the reign of George II the colony was sold to the Crown and the proprietary rights ceased. The first Royal Governor assumed his functions in 1731.

The population of New Bern in April 1775 was about six hundred. In 1792 there were about four hundred houses, all of wood excepting the Palace, the Church, the Gaol and two dwelling houses which were brick. By 1798, there were about 2000 people in the town and

ship building was carried on extensively. The ropes, iron work and timber were of home manufacture. The designers and craftsmen who found outlets for their talent in the shipyards seem to have worked also hand in hand with the guilds who wrought in brick and wood to provide a domestic architecture of great interest and beauty.

The first showplace of the town, Tryon's Palace, built in 1767, was designed by John Hawks, an architect who came to New Bern from the island of Malta. This three storied brick house with two storied wings, separated from the main building by curved colonnades, had a frontage of 87'-0" and a depth of 59'-0". £15,000 were raised by the people to pay the costs. Unfortunately it was burned in 1798 and only one wing is now standing. The absence of the "Palace," however, need not discourage the student and lover of early American architecture, for on almost every street one stands gratified in the presence of buildings which display real design and stunning craftsmanship.

New Bern contains such a wealth of architectural material that this first monograph will serve only as an introduction. I may mention here but a few selected examples.

The Groenendyke House, now known as the Hargett House, is a warm expression of ideals of comfort which the ancient merchants brought from Holland to our Carolina. One should not be surprised at the degree of preservation of these timbered homes. There were giant trees in those days; and only the eternal heart of them went into the making of colonial homes. Time was given to building them and no nails were used, where nails would disintegrate the fabric. Cozenly, an English walnut tree stands by the Groenendyke House and, at front, two crimson laurels, their trunks fluted and spiral; and a rose tree, growing there, it would seem, when the arch-mason of the Carpenters' Guild spent loving days of labor on this so nobly simple house. I think you will want to repeat the comfort and spaciousness of this apparently small house. The fireplace, you will surely want to repeat—I wonder whether we have added much to the things that really ease our weariness. Have we not abandoned the play of repose? I think great thoughts and tender fancies found food in the minds that clustered around the fireside in all our colonies. Well, anyway, our immortal men were to this manner born and reared. There was he who came out of Mt. Vernon; the Sage of Monticello; the great

much of his life in the gelid north but he has not found any scenes that this New Bern landside were ashamed to meet.

The "Louisiana" House, pictured below, stands facing the Neuse, and looking on to the south. Many a soulful watcher, I dare say, stood in the shade of that old gallery, looking for the homecoming of a seafaring father, or a shining-eyed and weather-beaten lover.

"LOUISIANA" HOUSE, EAST FRONT STREET, NEW BERN, NORTH CAROLINA

wood-chopper and his log cabin; Andrew Jackson's shack here in Carolina; Alexander Hamilton. Thanks be for the gathering love of ancient noble things.

There's little to choose between the climate of Louisiana and the coastal plain of North Carolina. So close are we to the fireside of the great Gulf Stream, that we do not shiver much here in winter; and in summer the breezes that come from the Neuse and the Trent, nights, sing "Always" to us. Fancy? Very well; take it so, if you will; but come and see. This writer lived

You should see the River Neuse, as it comes up almost to the feet of the "Louisiana" House. It is quite a mile and a half wide at this point; and as it moves on to the Sound, it widens and widens and widens. I seem to see it, a beautiful aisle, colonnaded by mossy water oaks, umbrella pines and mimosa trees.

What influences one in the "Louisiana" House are spaciousness and tonal effects. I just don't know how to tell these things technically; but I feel them and enjoy them thoroughly.

PRESBYTERIAN CHURCH, NEW BERN, NORTH CAROLINA

PRESBYTERIAN CHURCH, NEW BERN, NORTH CAROLINA

The Presbyterian Church is a noble building. The patrician portico is eloquent. Plato, likely, dictated his immortal sentences near columns such as these. The building is fifty-five feet in width and seventy feet in length with a steeple rising to a height of one hundred and twenty-five feet. Three doors open into an ample vestibule whence two open into the audience room. The pulpit is between the two doors at the entrance into the audience chamber. The floor gradually ascends toward the rear of the church elevating the pews to give a clear vision of the pulpit.

It is little wonder that we find the Jarvis (Slover) House and the Smallwood House, following so soon after the completion of this jewel of an early American Church. To architects, these houses must be luscious bits; to us laymen, beautiful works and gardens of repose. I think they are doing mighty much to tell our people that the builders of this Republic were not only political scientists; but men of poetic feeling and artistic expression. If I dared, I should almost say that they vied with their architects in fidelity to harmony and composition. The exquisite detail of these houses gives us to think that what they sought was not curtailment of cost, but rather the fulfillment of an ideal.

MASONIC OPERA HOUSE

Why those large and sculptured firesides? James Boyd, in "Drums," has a beautiful page that answers this question. Forensic art was developed there; classic lore had its chair there; political science was taught there.

When President George Washington came to New Bern in 1792, the Masonic Opera House was facing the Common, just as it is today. I do not know that I am reverent enough in speaking of this gracious old building, as quaint. I don't know that it represents any period; I do know it to be associated with the nobler sentiments of this community. One of its charms is the dignified lodge room on the upper floor.

A very "Kentucky Cardinal" of a Catholic priest lived in New Bern a hundred years ago. He had a very small congregation and was devoted to them. His love for his fellowman went out to the trees and song birds and his Irish terrier. It was such a person as this who built the little ridge-roofed house, with the delicate porch, you see illustrated at bottom of page 182.

The Hannah Clark House has distinction and articulation. Houses of this character are passed a hundred times unnoticed. Then they are discovered!

George III, the George who forced our Declaration of Independence, was represented here by an able, kindly and courteous governor—William Tryon. New Bern was the seat of government in Carolina. Governor Tryon built, what in 1768, was regarded as the most pretentious house in America. George Street began at the entrance of the Tryon Palace; went north—the King's Highway—to Kingston; and then on to the summer capital, Hillsboro, the farthest point north of the colony. Naturally, along this street worthy homes were built. One of these is the Hanff House. (See page 190).

Of a piece with the Hanff House, is the Blackwell House, now owned by G. C. Eubanks. This charming residence was built by Josiah Blackwell, in 1774. Josiah Blackwell was a lumber merchant, and into this construction, went materials of a beautiful texture.

The doorway of the Nixon House, is like a "Mammy Crochet" Rose—colorful and daintily reminiscent of the days of long ago; a fitting portal to a gracious interior. This house on Craven Street is the only remaining example, in this section of New Bern, of the elegant town house of the early nineteenth century period.

Athens was cultured, indeed; and made of her language a most fluid and beautiful speech; but she is known best for her Parthenon and her undying Acropolis.

HOUSE ON BROAD STREET, NEW BERN, NORTH CAROLINA

HOUSE AT 167 MIDDLE STREET, NEW BERN, NORTH CAROLINA

HANNAH CLARK HOUSE, CRAVEN STREET, NEW BERN, NORTH CAROLINA

BLACKWELL (TAYLOR) HOUSE, BROAD STREET, NEW BERN, NORTH CAROLINA

West Wall of the Masonic Lodge Room

MASONIC LODGE ROOM, NEW BERN, NORTH CAROLINA

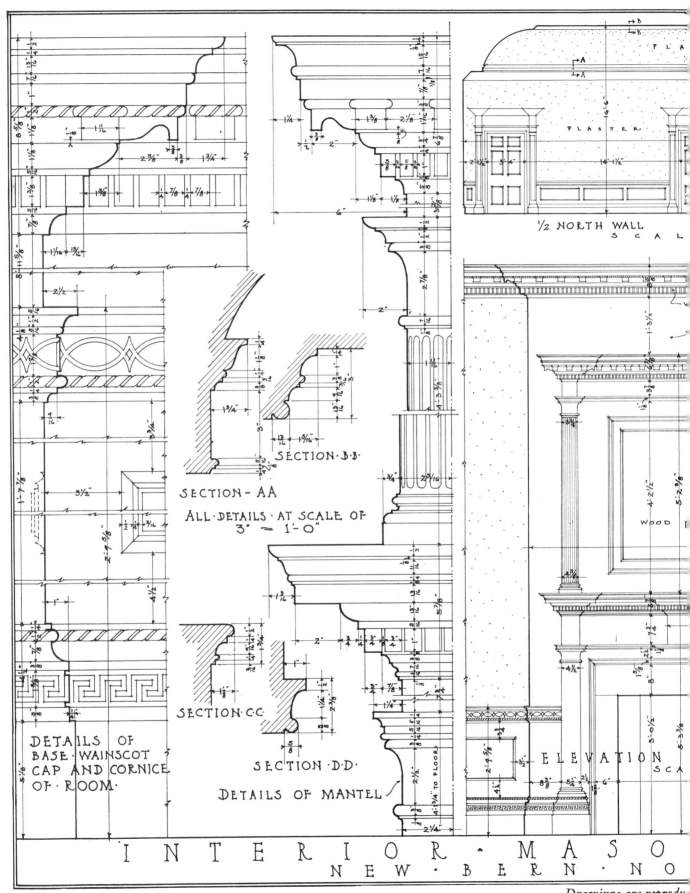

SECTION·B·B

SECTION - AA

ALL·DETAILS·AT SCALE OF
3" = 1'-0"

SECTION·C·C

SECTION·D·D

DETAILS OF MANTEL

DETAILS OF
BASE·WAINSCOT
CAP AND CORNICE
OF·ROOM.

½ NORTH WALL
SCALE

PLASTER

ELEVATION
SCALE

WOOD

INTERIOR · MASO
NEW · BERN · NO

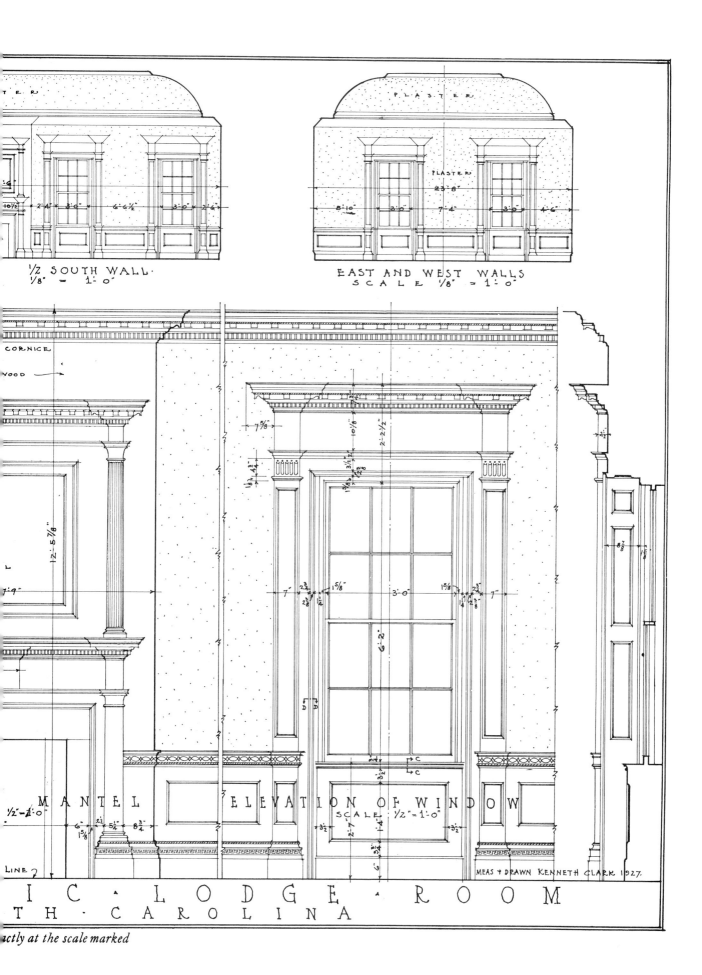

½ SOUTH WALL.
⅛" = 1'-0"

EAST AND WEST WALLS
SCALE ⅛" = 1'-0"

CORNICE

WOOD

MANTEL
½"=1'-0"

ELEVATION OF WINDOW
SCALE ½"=1'-0"

LINE

MEAS + DRAWN KENNETH CLARK 1927.

IC · LODGE · ROOM
TH · CAROLINA

actly at the scale marked

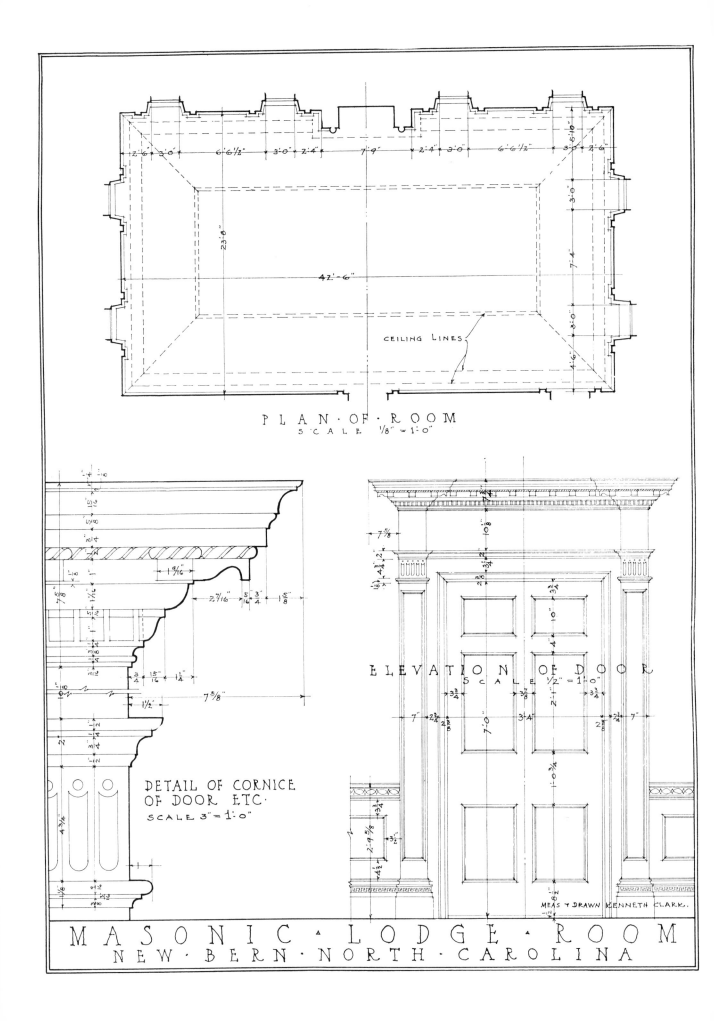

PLAN · OF · ROOM
SCALE ⅛" = 1'·0"

CEILING LINES

DETAIL OF CORNICE
OF DOOR ETC·
SCALE 3" = 1'·0"

ELEVATION OF DOOR
SCALE ½" = 1'·0"

MEAS ⊤ DRAWN KENNETH CLARK.

MASONIC · LODGE · ROOM
NEW · BERN · NORTH · CAROLINA

Detail of Door
MASONIC LODGE ROOM, NEW BERN, NORTH CAROLINA

HANFF HOUSE, GEORGE STREET, NEW BERN, NORTH CAROLINA

GAMBREL ROOF HOUSE, NEW BERN, NORTH CAROLINA

HOUSE ON HANCOCK STREET, NEW BERN, NORTH CAROLINA

HUGHES HOUSE, CRAVEN STREET, NEW BERN, NORTH CAROLINA
Torn down in 1925 and replaced by a garage!

NIXON HOUSE, CRAVEN STREET, NEW BERN, NORTH CAROLINA
Original steps removed when street was widened

Detail of Moulding
MASONIC LODGE ROOM, NEW BERN, NORTH CAROLINA

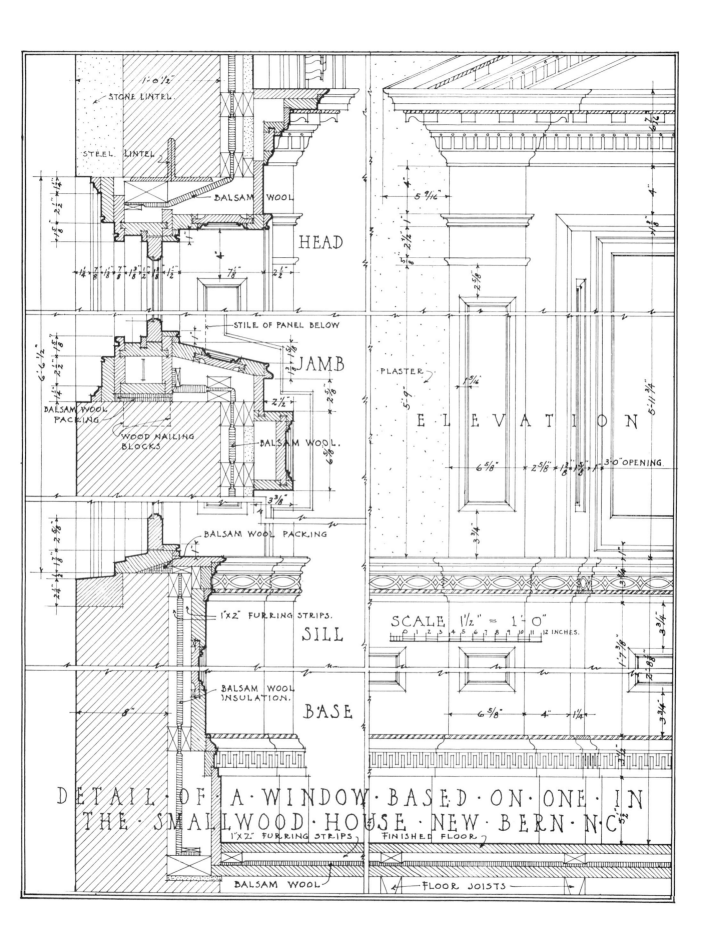

STONE LINTEL.

STEEL LINTEL

BALSAM WOOL

HEAD

STILE OF PANEL BELOW

JAMB

BALSAM WOOL PACKING

WOOD NAILING BLOCKS

BALSAM WOOL.

PLASTER

E L E V A T I O N

3'-0" OPENING

BALSAM WOOL PACKING

1"x2" FURRING STRIPS.

SILL

SCALE 1½" = 1'-0"
0 1 2 3 4 5 6 7 8 9 10 11 12 INCHES.

BALSAM WOOL INSULATION.

BASE

DETAIL · OF · A · WINDOW · BASED · ON · ONE · IN
THE · SMALLWOOD · HOUSE · NEW · BERN · N·C·

1"x2" FURRING STRIPS. FINISHED FLOOR

BALSAM WOOL FLOOR JOISTS

NIXON HOUSE, CRAVEN STREET, NEW BERN, NORTH CAROLINA

New Bern,
North Carolina
Part Two

Text by
Aymar Embury II
Photographs by
Kenneth Clark
Originally published in 1927 as White Pine Monograph
Volume XII, Number 2

JARVIS-SLOVER HOUSE, EAST FRONT STREET, NEW BERN, NORTH CAROLINA

NEW ENGLAND INFLUENCE ON NORTH CAROLINA ARCHITECTURE—NEW BERN, PART TWO

THE antiquary of early American architecture will usually find himself able by mere inspection of an old house or even of a photograph of one to tell with reasonable accuracy in which of the provinces it is built; and if his acquaintance with the old work is slightly more than casual, to give the date of its construction within five or ten years. Once in a while, however, he runs across a building or group of buildings which is exceedingly puzzling; if he knows the locality in which they occur, he cannot understand how they happened to be there; and he will in some cases be able to say of the time of construction only "they *ought* to date from about 17– to 17–, but I can't say in this case exactly when they were built."

These cases are the most fascinating in the study of our early architecture; just as with the collector it is the odd piece, the freak, that commands the highest price, so in architecture it is the unusual and unexpected that arrest the attention. The piece of design, no matter how fine, that is just the solution that one might have expected of that especial problem in its particular locality at the exact date it was built, may be greatly admired for its architectural qualities, but does not arouse curiosity as does the building which makes one wonder how? and why? There are found, for example, houses of genuine Colonial design in southern Ohio, and yet everybody knows that Ohio was not settled until long after the Revolution and that a Colonial house is as little to be expected there as a Jacobean one. In Elizabeth City there still exist, or did some years ago, the decaying remnants of the oldest bank in North Carolina, a stucco, tiled roof building, which shows strong Spanish or Provencal influence; one wonders if it was designed by some emigrant from New Orleans, or if it was erected in conformity with the memories of some Huguenot refugee from southern France.

Such another town is New Bern. One would expect to find its architecture a sort of provincial copy of the great metropolis of Williamsburg, Virginia on the north,

or (as Wilmington, N.C. indeed is) strongly flavored by the heavy beautiful Georgian of Charlestown; with the probability in favor of kinship with the Virginian type of Colonial, since North Carolina was settled rather through Norfolk than through Charlestown, and from the colonial period until today "the Carolinas" are much less allied to each other than North Carolina is with Virginia or South Carolina with Georgia. Actually we find its resemblance to either very slight indeed; but strangely enough, its lovely and elaborate houses, dating from the opening years of the nineteenth century would have passed without remark anywhere in New England of the late eighteenth, and they especially resemble the Salem of Samuel McIntire.

The illustrations in this chapter are sufficient and convincing evidence of the truth of this statement; but the causes of the resemblance (and these must have been compelling causes) are difficult or impossible to discover. In the similar case of the little hamlet of Clinton in southeastern Georgia, the local tradition provides a satisfactory solution. Clinton has only three or four houses of any size, all very much alike, and of a workmanship far superior to the average slovenly craftsmanship of the negro slaves who furnished the mechanics in the country districts of the south before the war. The detail is much less in scale than that in any of the surrounding districts, is far more elaborate, better designed, and distinctly earlier in feeling than the period at which it was built. Inquiry revealed that Clinton was settled about 1815 by emigrants from the northern part of Vermont, in which the Colonial tradition had not yet been superseded by that of the Greek revival, and where the intelligent and thorough craftsmanship of the colonial cabinet-maker still persisted. This hamlet became a sort of center for fine furniture; the few families from Vermont became wealthy from the products of their skill, and built for themselves houses as fine in design and probably larger than those they had left behind in Vermont; a few surviving chairs and tables of austere and delicate line, of maple or mahogany or walnut, scattered about Eastern Georgia reinforce the tradition.

No such definite evidence is available in the case of New Bern. On the contrary there are several confused, conflicting and indefinite traditions as to the designers of the old houses, and even with a good deal of research exact dates cannot be assigned to the buildings themselves. The customary statement is of course that they were all pre-Revolutionary; and that they were designed by Sir Christopher Wren or one of his pupils. Sir

civil work. This is plausible, but as the work bears no close resemblance to English Georgian and is very similar indeed to the late New England Colonial, the internal evidence would seem sufficient to give a negative answer to this tradition of derivation. It is of course possible that an English naval architect of some constructive skill and architectural imagination, called upon, in the absence of any more regularly trained architect, to design houses for his friends, would buy some books of design of American authorship and, following them as closely as he could, achieve approximately such houses as

JOHN WRIGHT STANLY HOUSE, NEW BERN, NORTH CAROLINA

Christopher Wren's pupils and George Washington's pew are the inevitable pleasant and ridiculous traditions current in all old towns and about all old churches; the mere fact that a church was built in 1810, while Wren died in 1723 and Washington in 1799, does not prevent the prideful custodian from pointing out the spire designed by Wren, and the pew occupied by Washington. The Washington tradition is feeble in New Bern but the Wren tradition is strong.

Another legend is that much of the later work was designed by an English architect, James Coor, who came to New Bern as a naval architect and branched out into

we find in New Bern. This is a sufficiently reasonable explanation, but based on a good many assumptions, any of which may be false; and if any one is false, the whole theory falls to the ground.

Another tradition is that the ships of New Bern departed on their voyages up the coast laden with leaf tobacco and molasses for the Salem factories to transform into smoking tobacco and rum for the pious New Englanders, and returned with furniture and woodwork, doors, mantels, and wainscot from the Salem makers. This again seems a perfectly tenable hypothesis, until we discover that the material of which the cabinet work

JARVIS-SLOVER HOUSE, EAST FRONT STREET, NEW BERN, NORTH CAROLINA

of New Bern is composed is not the northern white pine so beloved by the New England craftsman, but the native long leaf pine of North Carolina, and unless we assume that the ships which carried north the tobacco and molasses, carried long leaf pine timber to be worked up in New England, this pretty theory goes by the board. It is known that New Bern was in these early days and for many years thereafter a port from which much lumber was exported, and this may have happened; New England was already fairly well settled along the seaboard, and a lumber shortage was beginning to be felt; but even with due allowance for these things, it

merce of New Bern was largely with New England, and with Salem and Boston in particular, the New England architecture was seen, admired, and imitated. Certainly the designs are copied from the same handbooks used in New England, instead of the English books used further to the south; and New England mechanics may have acted as foremen and instructors. That is the case in many parts of the south today, and very likely was a hundred years ago.

Whatever its genesis, we can be grateful for the results obtained in this, the most prolific in good architecture of all the little cities of the south. The town fortu-

JUDGE DONALD HOUSE, 163 CRAVEN STREET, NEW BERN, NORTH CAROLINA
(From an old photograph by Wooten-Moulton Studio)

seems entirely improbable that New England mechanics would have used the hard brittle yellow pine for the complicated carvings so common in New Bern, when they could have and did procure for all their other work the soft, even-grained white pine.

One guess as to the origin of this lovely architecture is as good as another, — 'you pays your money and you takes your choice'; mine is that when the town began to grow rapidly, as it did just after the Revolution, it did what all other little cities did; used its local talent for design and construction, and the local talent used the books they could find most easily. Since the com-

nately escaped the vicissitudes of the Civil War, and preserved most of its old buildings intact; and since the population and wealth have grown very slowly during the last hundred years, it has also escaped that far more deadly enemy of fine old architecture, progress. Where are our old houses in New York and Philadelphia, or Boston? Those that still survive are museums or the homes of societies; but in New Bern they are still part of the daily life of the community; not thrust forward for admiration with "Do not touch" signs, on every corner, but used as they were intended to be, warm with human life and illumined with hospitality.

Entrance Detail
JUDGE DONALD HOUSE, NEW BERN, NORTH CAROLINA

Mantel Detail
JUDGE DONALD HOUSE, 163 CRAVEN STREET, NEW BERN, NORTH CAROLINA

Mantel Detail
WHITFORD HOUSE, 123 CRAVEN STREET, NEW BERN, NORTH CAROLINA

DUFFY HOUSE, NEW BERN, NORTH CAROLINA

Mantel, North Wall of Second Floor Drawing Room
SMALLWOOD HOUSE, NEW BERN, NORTH CAROLINA

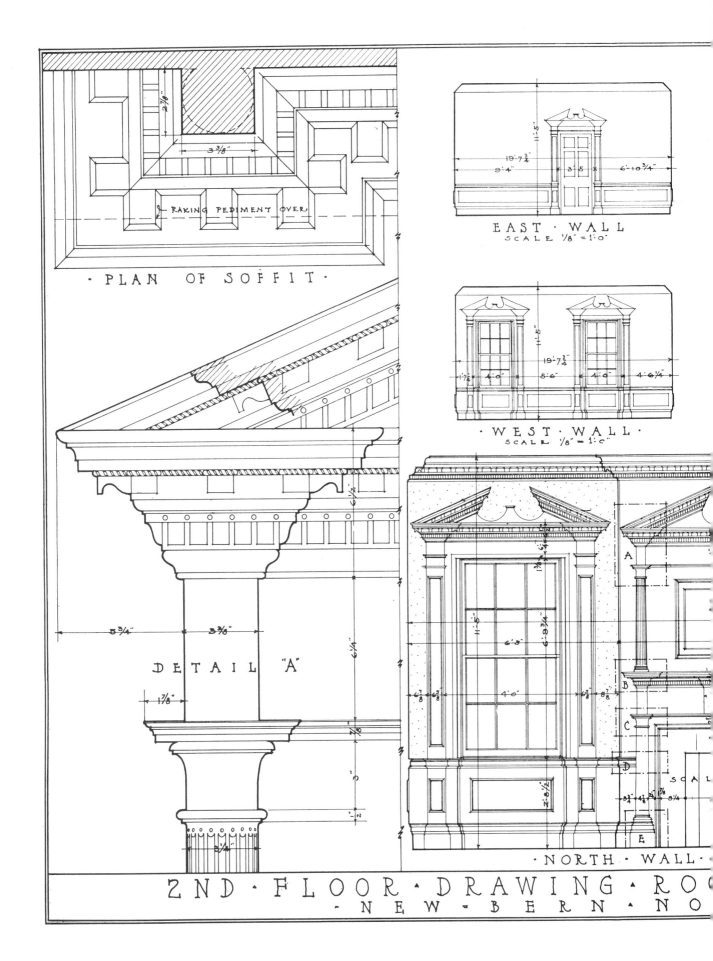

· PLAN · OF · SOFFIT ·

RAKING PEDIMENT OVER

EAST · WALL
SCALE 1/8" = 1'.0"

· WEST · WALL ·
SCALE 1/8" = 1'.0"

DETAIL "A"

· NORTH · WALL ·

2ND · FLOOR · DRAWING · ROO
· NEW · BERN · NO

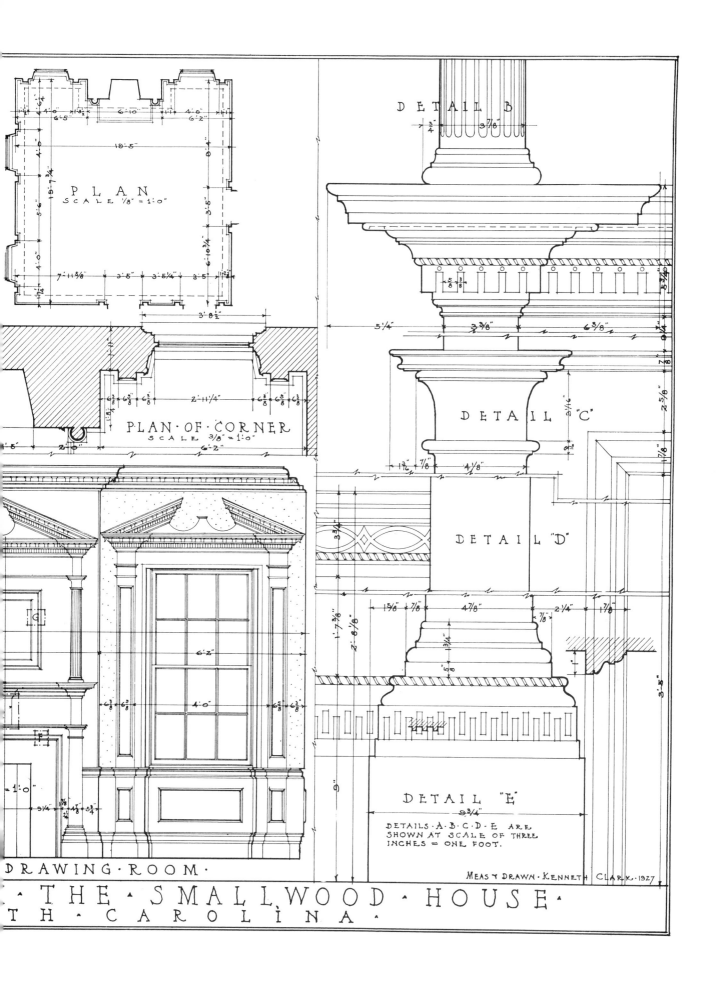

PLAN
SCALE 1/8" = 1'0"

PLAN · OF · CORNER
SCALE 3/8" = 1'0"

DETAIL B

DETAIL "C"

DETAIL "D"

DETAIL "E"

DETAILS · A · B · C · D · E · ARE
SHOWN AT SCALE OF THREE
INCHES = ONE FOOT.

· DRAWING · ROOM ·
· THE · SMALLWOOD · HOUSE ·
TH · CAROLINA ·

MEAS·Y·DRAWN·KENNETH·CLARK·1927

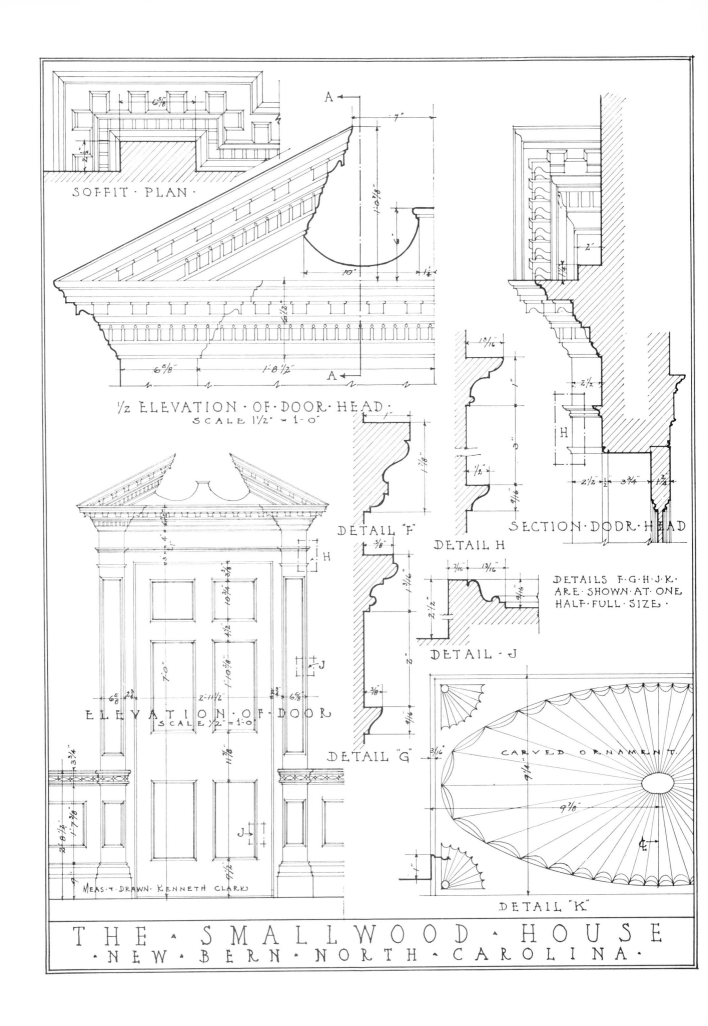

SOFFIT · PLAN ·

½ ELEVATION · OF · DOOR · HEAD ·
SCALE 1½" = 1-0"

DETAIL "F"

DETAIL H

SECTION · DODR · HEAD

DETAILS · F · G · H · J · K ·
ARE · SHOWN · AT · ONE ·
HALF · FULL · SIZE ·

DETAIL · J

DETAIL "G"

CARVED · ORNAMENT ·

ELEVATION · OF · DOOR
SCALE ½" = 1-0"

MEAS · + · DRAWN · KENNETH CLARK

DETAIL "K"

T H E · S M A L L W O O D · H O U S E
· N E W · B E R N · N O R T H · C A R O L I N A ·

Cornice Details
SMALLWOOD HOUSE, NEW BERN, NORTH CAROLINA

HOUSE ON CRAVEN STREET

STEVENSON HOUSE, POLLOCK STREET

TYPICAL HOUSES WITH "CAPTAIN'S WALK" AND ORNAMENTAL RAILING, NEW BERN, NORTH CAROLINA

ROBERTS HOUSE, NEW BERN, NORTH CAROLINA

HOUSE ON THE C.D. BRADHAM PROPERTY, NEW BERN, NORTH CAROLINA

LAW OFFICE ADJOINING THE JUDGE DONALD HOUSE, NEW BERN, NORTH CAROLINA

Stair
SMALLWOOD HOUSE, NEW BERN, NORTH CAROLINA

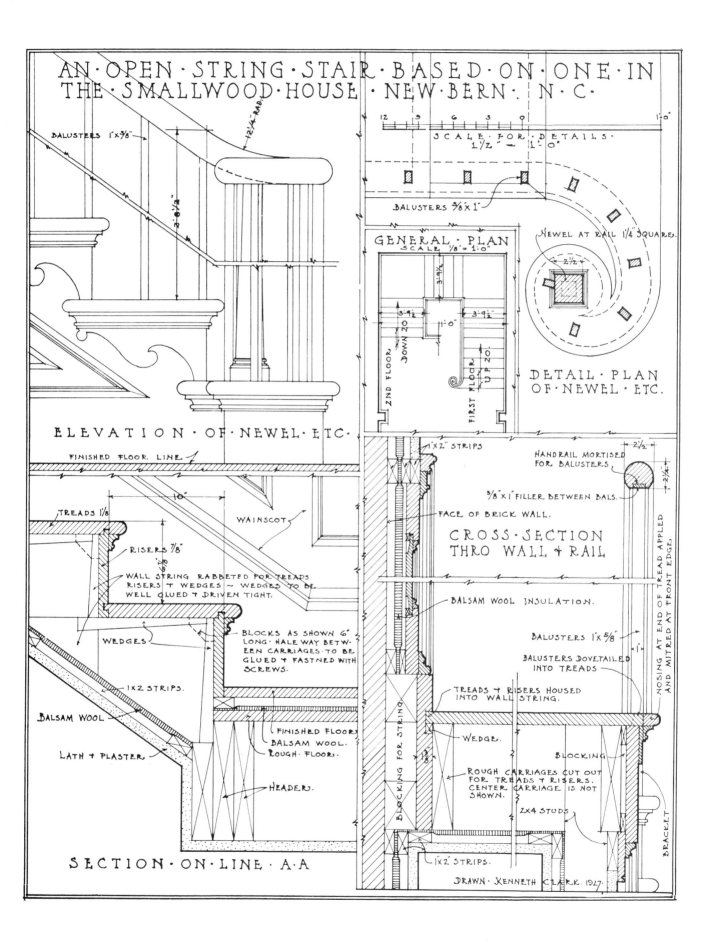

AN·OPEN·STRING·STAIR·BASED·ON·ONE·IN THE·SMALLWOOD·HOUSE·NEW·BERN·N·C·

BALUSTERS 1"X⅞"

12¼" RAD.

3'-0½"

ELEVATION·OF·NEWEL·ETC·

SCALE·FOR·DETAILS·
1½" = 1'-0"

BALUSTERS ⅝"X 1"

NEWEL AT RAIL 1¼" SQUARE.

2½

GENERAL·PLAN
SCALE ⅛" = 1'-0"

2ND FLOOR

3'-9½

DOWN 20

3'-9½

1'-0"

3'-9½

FIRST FLOOR

UP 20

DETAIL·PLAN
OF·NEWEL·ETC·

FINISHED FLOOR LINE

TREADS 1⅛"

RISERS ⅞"

9⅞"

WAINSCOT

10"

WALL STRING RABBETED FOR TREADS
RISERS & WEDGES ~ WEDGES TO BE
WELL GLUED & DRIVEN TIGHT.

WEDGES

1X2 STRIPS.

BLOCKS AS SHOWN 6"
LONG. HALF WAY BETW-
EEN CARRIAGES TO BE
GLUED & FASTNED WITH
SCREWS.

BALSAM WOOL

LATH & PLASTER

FINISHED FLOOR
BALSAM WOOL
ROUGH FLOOR

HEADER.

SECTION·ON·LINE·AA

1"X 2" STRIPS

HANDRAIL MORTISED
FOR BALUSTERS

2½

2¼"

⅜"X 1" FILLER BETWEEN BALS.

FACE OF BRICK WALL.

CROSS·SECTION
THRO WALL & RAIL

BALSAM WOOL INSULATION.

BALUSTERS 1"X ⅝"

BALUSTERS DOVETAILED
INTO TREADS

NOSING AT END OF TREAD APPLIED
AND MITRED AT FRONT EDGE.

1"

TREADS & RISERS HOUSED
INTO WALL STRING.

BLOCKING FOR STRING

WEDGE.

BLOCKING

1⅜

ROUGH CARRIAGES CUT OUT
FOR TREADS & RISERS.
CENTER CARRIAGE IS NOT
SHOWN.

2X4 STUDS

BRACKET

1"X 2" STRIPS.

DRAWN. KENNETH CLARK. 1927.

LAW OFFICE ADJOINING THE WASHINGTON BRYAN HOUSE, NEW BERN, NORTH CAROLINA

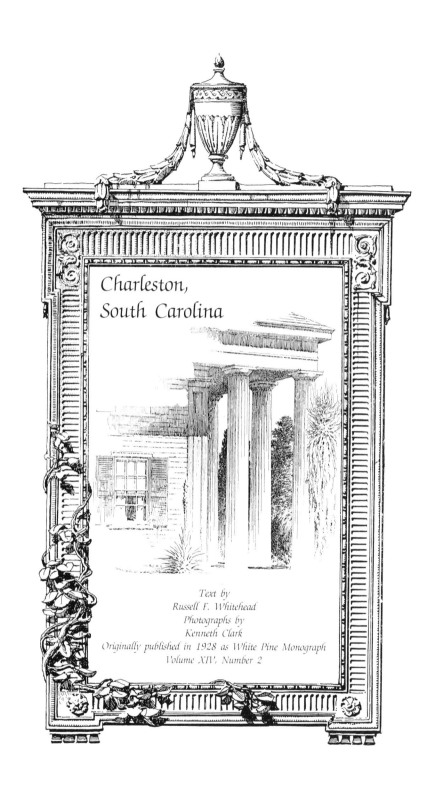

Charleston,
South Carolina

Text by
Russell F. Whitehead
Photographs by
Kenneth Clark
Originally published in 1928 as White Pine Monograph
Volume XIV, Number 2

ON CHURCH STREET, LOOKING TOWARD FIRST PRESBYTERIAN CHURCH,
CHARLESTON, SOUTH CAROLINA

THE CHARM OF OLD CHARLESTON
A NEW WORLD CITY OF OLD WORLD MEMORIES

ROMANCE, color and an atmosphere of the old world are depicted most vividly in subtropical Charleston. The student of architecture and the artist, alike, may experience the refreshment and tonic of a trip abroad as they poke about this beguiling old seaport and "summer resort" of Colonial America.

Fascinating vistas and compositions that are ever varied and delightful are seen throughout the city as one strolls up and down the narrow, mellow, old streets.

The Cavalier and the Huguenot left behind them a quaint mixture of English and French ideas of building and adornment, to which were added the influences of the San Dominican and West Indian settlers and the emigrants from the Low Countries of Europe. Their building is thoroughly adapted to the demands of the climate and the hospitable life of the Southern planter. The typical house is built on a line with the sidewalk, the narrow end and porch entrance on the street and enormous two or three story verandas facing on a side garden. High walls of brick and wood hide the gardens from the passer-by, but glimpses may be seen through the lacy patterns of the hand wrought iron gates.

The materials of construction are foreign in character. Brick, wood, Bermuda stone and oyster shell lime stucco in different colors, give a varied ensemble that is not at all consistent with the general idea of our early settlements. Salmon pink and purple black, moss spotted tile roofs add a subtle touch of color, as do the thick variegated slates and ancient shingles. The strange variety of roof intersections, unsymmetrical elevations, jutting wrought iron balconies and the way the buildings are placed in relation to the streets, make us feel that Charleston is the most "foreign" city in the United States.

Charleston justly claims an ancient and royal pedigree which through all the viscissitudes of two and a half centuries has left its stamp deeply imprinted. The ravages of two wars, in both of which this city played a conspicuous part, numerous general conflagrations and the earthquake of 1886 have caused the loss of many of her beautiful buildings. There is preserved, however, a wealth of uniquely interesting architecture. A comprehensive and accurate record of these buildings will be presented in this series as a part of the permanent record of early American architecture.

It has seemed to us that the buildings cannot be studied properly apart from their surroundings. To look comprehendingly up at church spires and splendid town houses, one must also look beyond them at the city and the people and the times that created them. To appreciate old Charleston at its fullest value it is necessary to see, not only the architectural monuments, but also their settings, and to catch the spirit and atmosphere of the place. It is for these reasons that we have selected the accompanying photographs as illustrations for the introductory chapter on Charleston. They will be a revelation to those who do not know the old town and an awakening of pleasant memories to those who do.

In the absence of any natural altitudes, the city lying on a peninsula as flat as a board between the two rivers, Ashley on the west and Cooper on the east, it is difficult to obtain a comprehensive view of the whole place. There are, however, many viewpoints hidden behind buildings or in the churchyards where it is impossible not to be moved by the lure of the surroundings. It does not require much imagination when walking through St. Michaels Alley or wandering in St. Philips graveyard to believe that America is three thousand miles away.

The visitor cannot escape the charm of Old Charleston—a charm which can only be suggested by Kenneth Clark's photographs and which we are privileged to reproduce. They will serve to recall to mind the extent of the debt our new world architecture owes to its European ancestry. Nowhere else in America, except possibly New Orleans and Quebec, can one discover a background so haunted by memories of the old world.

SPIRE OF ST. PHILIP'S CHURCH FROM GRAVEYARD OF THE HUGUENOT CHURCH,
CHARLESTON, SOUTH CAROLINA

MEETING STREET, ST. MICHAEL'S CHURCH AND SOUTH CAROLINA SOCIETY HALL,
CHARLESTON, SOUTH CAROLINA

GROUP OF BUILDINGS ON QUEEN STREET, CHARLESTON, SOUTH CAROLINA

GROUP OF BUILDINGS ON CHURCH STREET, CHARLESTON, SOUTH CAROLINA

ST. PHILIP'S CHURCH SPIRE FROM CHALMERS STREET, CHARLESTON, SOUTH CAROLINA

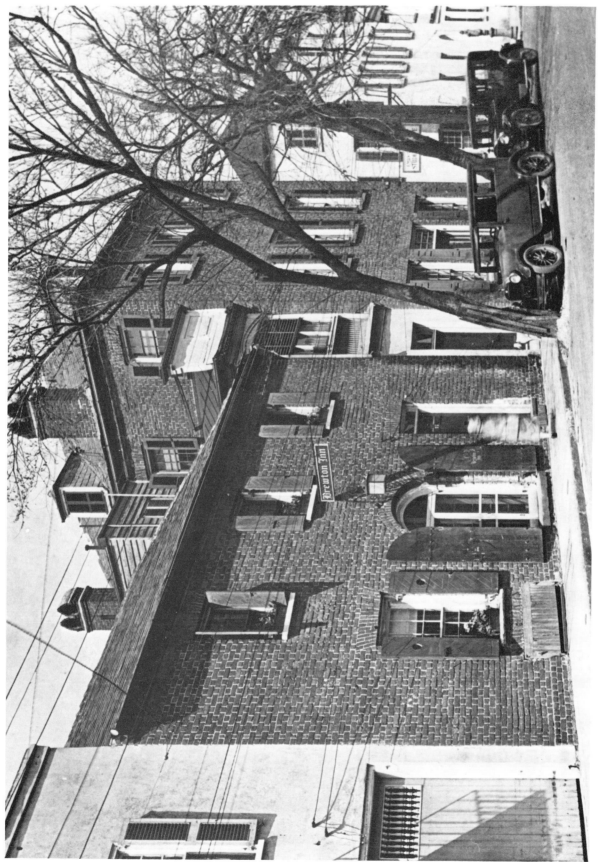

CHURCH STREET APPROACHING TRADD STREET – BREWTON – SAWTER HOUSE,
CHARLESTON, SOUTH CAROLINA

GROUP OF OLD HOUSES FROM ST. PHILIP'S CHURCHYARD, CHARLESTON, SOUTH CAROLINA

A TYPICAL HOUSE ON CHURCH STREET, CHARLESTON, SOUTH CAROLINA

ST. MICHAEL'S EAST LOOKING TOWARD MEETING STREET, CHARLESTON, SOUTH CAROLINA

ON CALHOUN STREET LOOKING TOWARD SECOND
PRESBYTERIAN CHURCH, CHARLESTON, SOUTH CAROLINA

Wall of the Graveyard
SECOND PRESBYTERIAN CHURCH, CHARLESTON, SOUTH CAROLINA

SERVANT'S QUARTERS OF DANIEL RAVENEL HOUSE AND WALL FROM WASHINGTON SQUARE,
CHARLESTON, SOUTH CAROLINA

Gateway
BLACKLOCK HOUSE, SOUTH CAROLINA

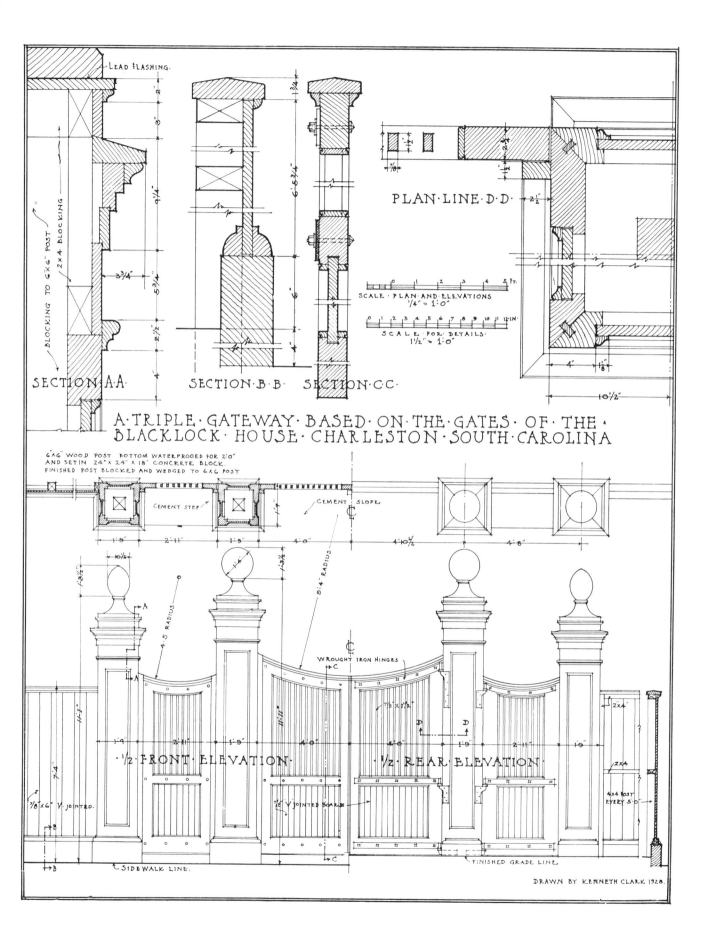

A·TRIPLE·GATEWAY·BASED·ON·THE·GATES·OF·THE·
BLACKLOCK·HOUSE·CHARLESTON·SOUTH·CAROLINA

LEAD FLASHING.

BLOCKING TO 6"×6" POST

2×4 BLOCKING

SECTION·A·A·   SECTION·B·B·   SECTION·C·C·

PLAN·LINE·D·D·

SCALE · PLAN · AND · ELEVATIONS
¼" = 1'·0"

SCALE · FOR · DETAILS ·
1½" = 1'·0"

6"×6" WOOD POST BOTTOM WATERPROOED FOR 2'·0"
AND SET IN 24"× 24"× 18" CONCRETE BLOCK.
FINISHED POST BLOCKED AND WEDGED TO 6×6 POST

CEMENT STEP

CEMENT SLOPE

WROUGHT IRON HINGES

½·FRONT·ELEVATION·   ½·REAR·ELEVATION·

⅞×6" V JOINTED.

⅞ V JOINTED BOARDS

2×4

2×4

4×4 POST
EVERY 5'·0"

SIDEWALK LINE.   FINISHED GRADE LINE.

DRAWN BY KENNETH CLARK 1928.

Gates
IZARD-EDWARDS-SMYTH HOUSE, 14 LEGARE STREET, CHARLESTON, SOUTH CAROLINA

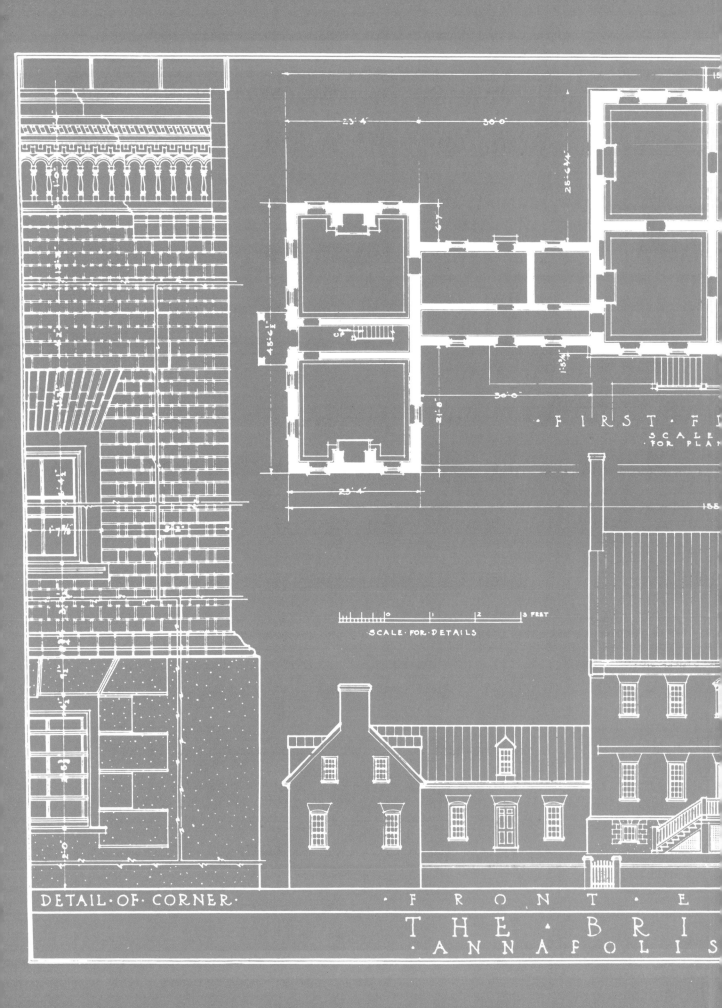

·SCALE·FOR·DETAILS·

·DETAIL·OF·CORNER·

·F R O N T · E

· T H E · B R I

· A N N A P O L I S